Teaching Law by
Design for Adjuncts

Teaching Law by Design for Adjuncts

SECOND EDITION

Sophie M. Sparrow

PROFESSOR, UNIVERSITY OF NEW HAMPSHIRE SCHOOL OF LAW,
CONSULTANT, INSTITUTE FOR LAW TEACHING AND LEARNING

Gerald F. Hess

PROFESSOR EMERITUS, GONZAGA UNIVERSITY SCHOOL OF LAW,
CONSULTANT, INSTITUTE FOR LAW TEACHING AND LEARNING

Michael Hunter Schwartz

DEAN AND PROFESSOR, UNIVERSITY OF ARKANSAS AT
LITTLE ROCK, WILLIAM H. BOWEN SCHOOL OF LAW,
CONSULTANT, INSTITUTE FOR LAW TEACHING AND LEARNING

CAROLINA ACADEMIC PRESS
Durham, North Carolina

Library of Congress Cataloging-in-Publication Data

Names: Sparrow, Sophie, author. | Hess, Gerald F., 1952- author. | Schwartz, Michael Hunter, author.
Title: Teaching law by design for adjuncts / Sophie Sparrow, Gerald F. Hess, and Michael Hunter Schwartz.
Description: Second edition. | Durham, North Carolina : Carolina Academic Press, 2017. | Includes bibliographical references and index.
Identifiers: LCCN 2016047009 | ISBN 9781611637021 (alk. paper)
Subjects: LCSH: Law--Study and teaching. | Law teachers--Vocational guidance.
Classification: LCC K100 .S68 2017 | DDC 340.071/1--dc23
LC record available at https://lccn.loc.gov/2016047009

CAROLINA ACADEMIC PRESS, LLC
700 Kent Street
Durham, North Carolina 27701
Telephone (919) 489-7486
Fax (919) 493-5668
www.cap-press.com

Printed in the United States of America

This book is dedicated to

My students, who constantly help me become a better teacher.
—Sophie

Adjunct professors, who have so much to offer our students.
—Gerry

My faculty colleagues at the UALR Bowen School of Law, both full-time and adjunct, who make me want to be a better law teacher and dean.

—Mike

Contents

Introduction   xv

Chapter 1 · What It Means to Be a Teacher   3
   What We Know about Effective Learning   3
     Cognitive Learning Theory   3
     Constructivist Learning Theory   5
     Adult Learning Theory   6
   What We Know about Effective Teaching   6
     Subject Matter Expertise   7
     Respect   7
     Expectations   8
     Support   8
     Passion   9
     Preparation and Organization   9
     Variety   10
     Active Learning   10
     Collaboration   11
     Clarity   11
     Formative Feedback   11

Chapter 2 · Student Perspectives on Teaching and Learning   13
   Students Want to Be Treated with Respect   13
     Use Students' Names   13
     Treat Students as Colleagues   14
     Include Different Perspectives in Class   14
     Create a Positive and Welcoming Environment   15
   Students Want to Be Engaged in Their Learning   16
     Use a Variety of Teaching Methods to Actively
      Engage Students   16

Give Students an Organizational Structure—
  Provide Context for Learning   17
Make Class Preparation Assignments Reasonable
  and Meaningful   17
Provide Opportunities for Students to Work
  with Others   18
Be Aware of Students' Concerns about the
  Socratic Method   19
Students Want to Become Good Lawyers   19
Connect What Students Are Learning to the
  Practice of Law   20
Be Explicit—Tell Students What You Expect and
  Give Them Opportunities to Practice   20
Give Students Feedback on Their Progress   21
Allow Students to Show Their Progress in
  Multiple Ways   22
Parting Shots—Students' General Advice to Us   22
How to Hear *Your* Students' Perspectives   23
Checklist for Considering the Students' Perspectives   23

Chapter 3 · Designing the Course   25
Introduction   25
Initiating the Design Process: Setting Course Goals   26
Know Your Students: Assessing the Learners   27
Plan Assessment: How Will You Know Whether
  Your Students Are Learning?   28
Finding the Book of Your Dreams: Sifting the
  Morass to Find the Right Textbook for You   28
Designing the Course So Students Will Learn What
  You Want Them to Learn   29
Writing Your Syllabus   32
Evaluate the Design and Plan for the Future   35
Checklist for Course Design Process   36

Chapter 4 · Designing Each Class Session   39
Context   39
Course Context   40
Student Context   40

Teacher Context   40
Class Objectives   41
    Learner Centered   41
    Professional Knowledge, Skills, and Values   41
    Clear and Concrete   42
Instructional Activities   43
    Opening   43
    Body   43
    Closing   45
Feedback   46
Materials   47
Evaluate and Revise   49
Checklist for Class Design Process   50

**Chapter 5 · Student Motivation, Attitudes, and
       Self-Regulation**   53
Introduction   53
Motivating Students   54
    Introduction   54
    Specific Techniques   55
Teaching for Attitude or Value Change or Development   58
    General Principles of Attitude Learning   58
    Techniques for Producing Attitude Change   59
Checklist for Teaching for Motivation and Attitude Change   64

Chapter 6 · Teaching the Class   65
Create a Positive Learning Environment Where
    Students Feel Safe Taking Risks   66
    Know and Use Students' Names   66
    Be Conscious of the Messages You Send   66
    Be Enthusiastic   67
    Model Taking Risks and Acknowledging Weaknesses   67
    Be Transparent and Authentic   68
The Nuts and Bolts   68
    Pre-Class: The 15 Minutes before Class Starts—
       Arrive Early   69
    Openings: The First Five Minutes of Class—Provide an
       Overview   69

Provide Students with the Objectives at the Beginning
of Class   69
See If Students Have Any Questions Arising from
the Previous Class Sessions   70
Administrative Matters   70
Modifications—First Day of the Course; Other
Significant Classes   71
The First Day of the Course   71
When Students Face Crises or Distractions   71
Body—The Heart of the Class Session   72
Focus on One to Three Learning Objectives per
One-Hour Class Session   72
Active Learning Exercises   73
Additional Points about Instructional Activities   77
Lectures   77
Use Micro-Lectures—10 to 15 Minutes   77
Add Valuable Content   78
Surround Micro-Lectures with Other Activities   78
Include Visuals   78
Deliver Micro-Lectures Effectively   78
Questioning Techniques   79
Prepare Students in Advance   79
Ask Clear Questions   80
Ask One Question at a Time   80
Ask a Range of Questions   80
Allow Sufficient Wait-Time (at Least Three to
Five Seconds) after You Ask a Question   81
Encourage and Promote Effective Responses, Respond
Appropriately to Ineffective Answers   81
Visuals   82
PowerPoint and Other Visuals   82
Dress   83
Discovery Sequence Instruction   84
Timing   85
Closings: The Last Five Minutes of Class   86
Summarize Key Points   86
Give Students Time to Consolidate Their Learning   87

Allow Students to Reflect on Their Learning 87
Closing Modification: The Very Last Class—Leave Ten
to Fifteen Minutes for the Final Closing 88
Final Notes on Teaching the Class 88
Checklist for Teaching the Class 89

Chapter 7 · Experiential Teaching and Learning 91
Introduction 91
Experiential Exercises and Methods 92
Specific Examples of Experiential Exercises 94
1. Current Events and Real-Life Stories 94
2. Documents—Reading and Reviewing 95
3. Documents—Drafting 96
4. Field Trips 96
5. Guest Speakers 97
6. Interviews 98
7. Problem-Solving 98
8. Short Role Plays 99
9. Simulations 100
10. Student Presentations 101
Designing Experiential Exercises and Methods 102
Considerations for Designing Experiential Exercises 102
1. Focus on Learning Goals and Objectives 103
2. Choose the Experiential Method/s 103
3. Design the Overall Structure 103
4. Find Relevant and Significant Material 104
5. Provide Clear Goals, Directions, and Expectations 104
6. Identify What You Have to Do to Adequately
Prepare for the Exercise 106
7. Identify What Students Have to Do to Adequately
Prepare for the Exercise 106
8. Determine What Feedback Students Will Receive 106
9. Determine Whether Students Will Reflect Upon
the Exercise 107
10. Reflect and Self-Assess the Experience 107

Chapter 8 · Deep, Lasting Learning 111
What Is Exceptional, Significant, Lasting Learning? 111

How Can Teachers Foster Deep, Lasting Learning for
Students?   113
Choose Learning Objectives That Address Significant,
Lasting Learning   113
Create a Challenging, Supportive, Collaborative
Teaching and Learning Environment   116
Engage Students in Rich, Textured Learning Activities 117
Incorporate Frequent Formative Feedback   121

Chapter 9 · Assessing Student Learning   125
Introduction   125
Step One: Identify Learning Objectives   125
Step Two: Prepare the Assessment Instrument   126
Step Three: Give Feedback to Students   129
Using Classroom Assessment Techniques to Improve
Your Teaching   132
Evaluating Students to Assign Grades—The Hardest
Part of Assessment   133
Essential Elements   133
The Grading Process Itself—Designing and Using
Rubrics/Scoring Sheets—One Way   136
Checklist for Assessing Student Learning   137

Chapter 10 · Troubleshooting   141
Challenge 1: Unprepared or Unmotivated Students   141
The Challenge   141
Addressing the Challenge   142
Challenge 2: Disrespectful Students   143
The Challenge   143
Addressing the Challenge   143
Challenge 3: Getting Lackluster or Poor
Student Evaluations   145
The Challenge   145
Addressing the Challenge   146
Challenge 4: Doing Multiple Assessments without
Killing Yourself   147
The Challenge   147
Addressing the Challenge   148

Challenge 5: Addressing Controversial Topics in Class 149
    The Challenge 149
    Addressing the Challenge 149
Challenge 6: Being Asked a Question That You Are
    Unable to Answer in the Moment or Making a
    Mistake in Class 152
    The Challenge 152
    Addressing the Challenge 153
Challenge 7: Students Do Not Read: (1) The Instructions
    on Exams, (2) Assignment Instructions, (3) Emails,
    or (4) the Syllabus 154
    The Challenge 154
    Addressing the Challenge 154
Conclusion: Common Themes 155

Chapter 11 · Developing as a Teacher 157
Sustaining a Teaching Practice 157
Self-Assessment, Reflection, and Study 159
    Benefits of Reflective Practice 159
    Self-Assessment 160
    Teaching Journal 160
    Print and Electronic Resources 162
Formative Feedback from Students 162
    Student Evaluations 162
    Feedback from Students during the Course 163
Collaborating with Colleagues 165
    Discussions with Colleagues 165
    Peer Observations and Feedback 165
Consultants 166
Teaching Workshops and Conferences 168
Checklist for Teaching Development 169

Selected Resources—Books, Articles, Newsletters,
    Videos, and Websites 171

About the Context and Practice Series 175

Index 177

Introduction

Our primary goal in this book is to provide concrete suggestions for adjunct professors about how to design and conduct all
aspects of teaching law students, based on the enormous body of
research on teaching and learning. New and experienced adjuncts
can apply the book's principles from sequencing a course to grading an exam.

We hope the book helps you and your students enjoy teaching
and learning in law school. At the same time, we caution you not
to feel compelled to adopt every suggestion in this book. Not only
has none of us adopted every suggestion in this book, but we
doubt anyone could do so. Instead, make small rather than wholesale changes, evaluate the effectiveness of every new practice you
try, keep doing the things that work, discard the things that don't
work, and, above all, aspire to continuous improvement.

The first chapter provides a legal education-focused overview
of the research on teaching and learning. The second chapter cap-
tures the student perspective on law teaching and learning. Chapters 3 through 10 focus on fundamental elements of teaching and
learning: course design, class design, student motivation, teaching
methods, experiential exercises, lasting learning, troubleshooting,
and assessment. Chapter 11 focuses on things law teachers can do
to systematically improve themselves as teachers.

All of the chapters and accompanying appendices from the first
edition of this book have been substantially revised and updated.
The chapters on experiential learning, lasting learning, and troubleshooting are new. Most chapters are directly applicable to all law
teachers, courses, and students, but four chapters focus primarily
on doctrinal courses (Chapter 6—teaching the class, Chapter 7—

experiential learning, Chapter 9—assessment, and Chapter 10—troubleshooting).

We hope that this book will be a valuable resource for adjunct professors. We recommend four other important recourses to help adjuncts excel as teachers.

The first resource is the Appendix for this book and for *Teaching Law by Design: Engaging Students from the Syllabus to the Final Exam,* Second Edition (a more detailed version of this book). The Appendix has many examples of syllabi, exercises, handouts, grading rubrics, and other documents related to the material in this text. The Appendix is available for free on the website of the Institute for Law Teaching and Learning at http://lawteaching.org/resources/books/teachinglawbydesign/teachinglawbydesign-appendices.pdf.

The second resource is the American Bar Association's *Adjunct Faculty Handbook* (2005). This 47-page document contains helpful advice on preparing to teach, conducting the class, grading, and working with your law school. The *Handbook* is free and available on the ABA's website at http://www.abanet.org/legaled/publications/adjuncthandbook/adjuncthandbook.pdf.

A third resource is the faculty at the school where you teach. Other adjuncts and full-time faculty can provide a wealth of information about teaching, brainstorm ideas with you, and help you trouble shoot challenges.

Finally, the associate dean at your law school is a critical resource. The associate dean will be familiar with your law school's policies, resources, programs, and culture. It is important for you to know your school's policies and rules before you begin teaching. We encourage you to develop a strong working relationship with your associate dean. Understanding your associate dean's expectations will help you avoid common problems the associate dean may have encountered in the past. If the associate dean is unable to address your questions directly, she may provide you with a list of other faculty you can use as a resource. As part of our research for this book, we asked associate deans for their advice for adjunct professors. Four themes emerged in their advice: (1) be prepared to work hard—many adjuncts underestimate the difficulty of teaching a law school course; (2) develop objectives for your courses and class sessions; (3) establish and maintain a respectful, challenging classroom environment; and (4) comply with the school's grading policies and deadlines. We agree with this advice and believe that this book will help you meet and exceed the expectations of your associate dean.

While we wrote this book in an effort to share what we believe to be core principles of teaching and learning, the book also is sort of a white paper for the Context and Practice Casebook series from Carolina Academic Press. The series is designed to apply the principles from this book, as well as other insights and recommendations from *Best Practices in Legal Education* (Clea 2007) and *Educating Lawyers* (Jossey-Bass 2007), to the creation of law school course materials.

We wish to thank the many people who made this book possible. We appreciate the support of our law schools, our students, our families, and the helpful folks at Carolina Academic Press.

Sophie M. Sparrow
University of New Hampshire School of Law
Consultant, Institute for Law Teaching and Learning

Gerald Hess
Gonzaga University School of Law
Consultant, Institute for Law Teaching and Learning

Michael Hunter Schwartz
University of Arkansas at Little Rock, William H. Bowen School of Law, Consultant, Institute for Law Teaching and Learning

Teaching Law by
Design for Adjuncts

Chapter 1

What It Means to Be a Teacher

This chapter explores what we know about effective learning and effective teaching.

What We Know about Effective Learning

We have chosen to start a book on teaching with what we know about effective learning. That choice is deliberate. Teaching is effective only if it produces significant learning. Significant learning, whether labeled "mastery" or "competency," is the ability to use what one has learned. Thus, law students have learned something significant when they can use their legal skills and knowledge to solve a legal problem.

Cognitive Learning Theory

According to "cognitive theory," students cannot apply skills and knowledge unless they have stored what they learned in an organized, meaningful and useable way. The processes of storing new learning and retrieving stored learning occur according to the sequence depicted below in Illustration 1-1. Although the sequence may appear linear, moving from one place to the next, the process probably is more circular and interactive. Although we describe this "cognitive processing" as a model or theory, considerable research supports its accuracy.

Hundreds of pieces of information reach our students' senses every moment. Humans can attend, however, to only a few of

Illustration 1-1. A Model of Cognitive Processing

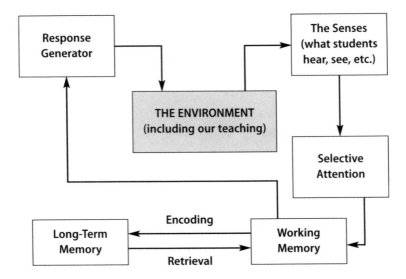

these pieces of information so our students must decide: which stimuli warrant attention? The process of choosing a focus is known as "selective attention." Thus, the learning process is over at the spigot if our students decide to pay attention to their e-mail or their eBay purchases. Of course, all we hear is, "What was the question?"

If our students do pay attention, what we teach passes into their working memory. Students' working memory can retain only a small amount of learning and only for a limited time. But when our students do something *active* to store their learning in a meaningful way, the information becomes a part of their long-term memory.

For this reason, engaging students in active learning activities is crucial to learning. Active learning activities are those in which students cannot simply sit and listen but must do something to mentally process the concepts we want them to learn. If students are writing about the concepts, discussing them with a peer, fig-uring out how they relate to each other and to what they already know, students are engaged in active learning. Moreover, the more deeply students think about what they are learning, the more likely they are to remember and use it.

But storing learned skills and knowledge isn't enough. To analyze a problem, students must recall ("retrieve") what they have learned and use that learning to interact with the environment in some way.

Constructivist Learning Theory

Consequently, constructivist theory focuses on the process required for new learning to become a more-or-less permanent part of who the students are. Three crucial learning principles derive from constructivist research. First, learning is a matter of constructing an interpretation from an experience. When students engage with materials in an active, effortful way and reflect on the process, they develop personal understandings. And those personal understandings, having been entirely generated within the student's mind, stay with the student. Thus, significant law student learning only can happen if the students have opportunities to develop such interpretations, to figure things out for themselves.

Constructivists also emphasize the importance of real-world experiences, both in learning activities and assessment. Students learn when their opportunities to construct understandings are authentic, such as when their learning is anchored in a realistic context. Thus, law professors who teach cases and rules in the context of law practice problems, whether simulations or actual client issues, provide students the authenticity they need to construct meaningful understandings.

Finally, constructivists emphasize the role of social interaction in learning. Students engage in crucial mental activity when they negotiate meaning with each other. The hundreds of studies demonstrating the superiority of cooperative learning groups compared to all other teaching methods support this assertion. These groups are so effective because they allow students to obtain access to multiple perspectives with respect to a problem or issue and thereby to develop the more complex approaches and understandings required to address complicated problems.

Of course, such results are the product of groups who know how to work together, how to subdue ego in service of the goal of obtaining the best results possible, how to develop "positive interdependence," where each member of the group invests in the success of every other member of the group, and how to develop "accountability," where each member of the group holds every other member of the group responsible for performing her or his share of the group work. Chapter 6 addresses best practices for creating productive small group projects.

Adult Learning Theory

Adult learning theory has considerable overlap with both the cognitive and constructivist theories. First, like constructivism, adult learning theory emphasizes the importance of real world experiences, but adult learning theory takes this idea one step further: not only must the experience be authentic, but the students must see the experience as authentic *and* as important to their personal and professional needs. Moreover, while adult learning theory and cognitivist theory share an emphasis on articulating learning goals, adult learning theory teaches us that students not only want to know what they need to be learning and how what they are learning relates their career goals, but also want to understand the relationship between the learning goals and the methods the teacher has chosen to achieve those goals. Like both cognitivism and constructivism, adult learning theory emphasizes the need for students to be in control of their own learning process. Students must have a role in deciding what and how they will learn. Finally, adult learning theory emphasizes the importance of teachers manifesting their respect for their students.

What We Know about Effective Teaching

Based on the research about teaching effectiveness in higher education, teaching excellence is measured by significant student learning. Teachers facilitate significant student learning when their teaching practices include expertise, respect, expectations, support, passion, preparation, variety, active learning, collaboration, clarity, and formative feedback.

Subject Matter Expertise

An essential foundation of good teaching is subject matter expertise. To teach well, we need to know doctrine, theory, policy, practical application, thinking skills, performance skills, ethical issues, and professionalism.

Respect

Mutual respect among students and teachers is fundamental to a healthy teaching and learning environment. Respect should go in three directions: teacher to students, students to teacher, and students to students. Classrooms that feature humiliation, intimidation, or denigration lead many students to withdraw from participation and learning.

Here's a brief list of behaviors that foster respect.

- Learn your students' names. Call students by name in and out of the classroom.
- Learn about your students' experiences and goals. Have students introduce themselves by completing a short questionnaire in class or on line.
- Value students' time. Law students, like their teachers, lead busy lives. Start and end class on time. Keep appointments with students. Respond to email from students.
- Be inclusive. We motivate students when we make them feel welcome and when we try to tie their learning to their personal and professional interests.
- Model respect. Respect is more about what we do than what we say. It is how we treat students, colleagues, and staff on a daily basis.

Expectations

Teachers' expectations greatly affect students' learning. High, realistic expectations lead to more student achievement; low expectations result in less student learning.

Five attributes of teacher expectations affect student motivation and learning: clarity, quality, achievability, uniformity, and credibility. Clarity requires us to define our expectations for both ourselves and our students. Quality means we need to emphasize quality rather than quantity. No course can teach all the skills and knowledge students need to develop; consequently, we should emphasize the critical skills and knowledge and accept we cannot teach everything. Achievability means our expectations should challenge students to stretch themselves and to do their best work while accounting for our students' current level of level of development and the demands of professional practice. Expectations are uniform if we communicate that we believe every student can attain a high level of achievement. Finally, our expectations are credible if we impose high expectations on ourselves. Perhaps the best way for teachers to inspire students to excellence is through modeling. We should have high expectations for ourselves. We should show, day after day, that we are diligently seeking continuous improvement in our professional practice.

Support

A supportive teaching and learning environment should accompany high expectations. We should demonstrate our commitment to helping each student succeed in law school. A supportive environment is built upon teachers' attitudes, availability, and trust.

One set of common descriptors of exemplary teachers focuses on their attitudes toward students—"helpful," "caring," "concerned," and "encouraging." Another group of attributes of effective teachers is "available," "accessible," and "approachable." Student-faculty contact outside of formal class time is associated with students' motivation, satisfaction, and active involvement in their own education. An operating assumption that reflects our trust is that "there is a good faith explanation for students' behavior." When we communicate our faith in students, most will reciprocate with faith in us.

Passion

Students regularly identify teachers' passion or enthusiasm as the most important ingredient of effective instruction. Our passion can inspire, energize, and motivate our students.

We should tell students directly what we love about teaching at this school, our joy in working with students, and our fascination with the subject matter. Celebrate success in the classroom. Provide positive reinforcement when students produce insight, solid analysis, or creative thinking. Teachers' nonverbal behaviors associated with enthusiasm include movement (away from the podium and out into the classroom), gestures, facial expressions, and smiling.

Preparation and Organization

Teachers and students benefit when they are clear about what should be learned, how that learning will take place, and how students will demonstrate their learning.

Preparation on the course design level includes: assessing our students' incoming strengths and weaknesses; establishing expectations for student attendance, preparation, participation, and behavior; planning our teaching methods, exercises, and assignments, both in and out of class; selecting print and electronic resources that will support the teaching and learning activities; pacing the course rather than letting the clock or the calendar determine how fast and what we teach; designing opportunities for feedback to students throughout the course; and, of course, determining how student performance will be assessed and graded. Chapter 3 is devoted to course design.

A parallel set of issues inform our design of individual class sessions. Class session design includes: assessing where the students are at this point in the course in terms of their understanding and skills; selecting two, three, or four concepts or skills that students should learn or practice in the class session; deciding what students should do outside of class to prepare; planning what students will do during class; consciously choosing how the session will begin and end; and planning opportunities for teacher and student feedback about the students' learning. Chapter 4 addresses class session design.

Effective teachers are not only prepared and organized; they are flexible too. Planning need not lead to rigidity. In every course and many individual class sessions, opportunities present themselves to explore a concept in more depth, weave in professionalism, and build on students' insights and skills.

Variety

We can inject variety into many aspects of our teaching—objectives, teaching and learning methods, materials, and evaluation. The extensive literature on learning style preferences makes clear that students prefer to learn in different ways. In addition, different types of teaching methods and materials are appropriate to achieve different objectives. Variety can keep students' interest and sustain their motivation throughout a course.

Active Learning

Students learn from active and passive methods. Students learn passively when they listen to a presenter who organizes and conveys information. Active learning occurs when students engage in more than listening. Law teachers employ many types of active learning techniques: Socratic dialogs, discussions, writing exercises, simulations, computer exercises, and real-life experiences in externships and clinics. Active learning is particularly effective in achieving core goals of legal education, including thinking skills, legal doctrine, lawyering skills, and professional values.

Collaboration

A large body of research in higher education and legal education documents the effectiveness of cooperative learning, where students work in pairs or small groups in or outside of class. Cooperative learning fosters the following: (1) more student learning and better academic performance, especially when the task is complex and conceptual; (2) development of problem solving, reasoning, and critical thinking skills; (3) positive student attitudes toward the subject matter and course; (4) closer relationships among students and between students and teachers; and (5) students' willingness to consider diverse perspectives.

Clarity

Clarity in the classroom is *not* about "spoonfeeding" or "dumbing-down." Instead, it is about effectively communicating complex ideas, skills, and professional values. Several practices can help us communicate more clearly in the classroom, including roadmaps, closure, examples, visuals, and manifested openness to student questions.

Formative Feedback

Feedback is a critical element of teaching and learning. Formative feedback, which is designed to improve learning, is an essential part of the learning loop. Students engage in learning activities, show their learning in writing or orally, and then get feedback on how to improve their learning and performance. Effective formative feedback has four characteristics: specific, corrective, positive, and timely. Teachers should articulate *specific* criteria for student performance and give students feedback based on those criteria. *Corrective* feedback points out weaknesses in student work and provides strategies for improvement. *Positive* feedback identifies the strengths upon which students can build. *Timely* feedback comes relatively soon after student performance and gives students an opportunity to improve before their performance is evaluated.

Formative feedback is essential for teachers' continued development as well. To make appropriate adjustments during a course, we need to get feedback from students about their learning. A variety of Classroom Assessment Techniques (see Chapter 9) can give us that feedback. Further, for continuous improvement of our teaching practice, we can engage in self-reflection and gather input from students, consultants, and colleagues (see Chapter 11).

Chapter 2

Student Perspectives on Teaching and Learning

[T]o have the honor of being called a teacher-professor, you need to educate yourself about how to be an effective teacher.

Because good teaching focuses on student learning, we have included students' views about their legal education. **Students ask us to treat them with respect, engage them in learning, and help them become good lawyers.** They do not ask us to lower our expectations or "dumb down" their experience. In this chapter, we offer you students' words (in italics), mostly excerpts of students' comments taken from sixteen hours of videotaped interviews with sixty-seven students from seven different law schools. For ways to implement specific suggestions, see Chapters 3, 4, 5, 6, 7, 8 and 9.

Students Want to Be Treated with Respect

I learn better from professors that I feel talk with me and not down to me.

Students want us to treat them with compassion, welcome their different perspectives, create a positive and welcoming environment, and use their names. Respect is critical in the law school classroom.

Use Students' Names

[W]hen you raised your hand, it was not you in the back or you with the shirt, it was Ms. So and So or Mr. So and So.

And it absolutely made you feel like all right the focus is on me and this professor wants to hear what I'm about to say.

Using students' names shows great respect. Students are delighted when teachers know their names and pronounce them correctly. Even if we can't learn all the names of our students in class, we can still have them available, on "name tents" placed in front students, on a seating chart, and we can use them in class discussions.

Treat Students as Colleagues

[I]t's not necessary for the professor to impress me by speaking in a mysterious language.... I'm already in awe of the professors. But I want to learn from a human being, a fellow human being.

Students frequently note that they learn more effectively from teachers whom they feel treat them as novice colleagues and who acknowledge their own fallibility. Our humanity empowers and motivates them; it does not make us appear weak. Being able to laugh at ourselves, admit mistakes, and acknowledge emotions help our students connect with us.

Include Different Perspectives in Class

I would advise a new professor [to] remember that he is teaching a group of people with varying cultural experiences and to actively solicit varying opinions so that the class is not dominated by a single culture.

Students want us to recognize how many different perspectives there are in the classroom, and seek to learn more about them. They want us to be willing to talk about difficult issues of race, gender, sexual orientation and identification, religion, and politics. They want us to realize that our references to sports and culture may be meaningless to them. On the other hand, diverse students may not want to be "spokespeople" for a certain perspective.

I'm in Criminal Law class where being one of two minority students in the class it seemed that every time that an issue of race came up that for some instant the professor always called on me as if I was the answer, you know, to everything. And sometimes I didn't mind it but then sometimes I did mind it because I didn't feel as though my purpose for being in that class was to answer all race issues that came up within that class.

Create a Positive and Welcoming Environment

Teachers' and classmates' negative comments threaten students' confidence in their ability to grasp difficult material. They want us to maintain an enthusiastic, encouraging, and professional atmosphere.

I tend to learn better from professors that I respect and create that environment and make me feel that I can contribute to the profession. [W]hen [teachers] don't check a student that is talking out of line … or if they don't maintain that kind of decorum … it's very distracting to others … since this is a professional environment … there is a duty that teachers have of maintaining that.

Creating a positive environment means that we also need to be careful about the assumptions we make about students.

[A]t least 99% [of us] try our hardest to make sure that we get it because we don't want to look foolish in class…. [I]t's very important that a teacher realize that … we wouldn't ask the question in class … unless we just honestly didn't understand it.

Students Want to Be Engaged in Their Learning

The vast majority of students come to law school excited about becoming lawyers. They want assignments that relate to what happens in class. They seek to understand where the class is going and what they should take away at the end. Students want to be engaged in class. To help engage your students, ask not what **you** are doing, but what **they** are doing.

Use a Variety of Teaching Methods to Actively Engage Students

> [T]he more variation you can bring to class the more interested ... I stay. When it's just strictly lecture I tend to have a habit of drifting in and out.

Having a variety of teaching methods allows students to learn things in different ways, reaches students' diverse learning preferences, helps students solve legal problems from new angles, and mixes up the usual class performance patterns.

> [What] really helps in the process of the day-to-day going to class and getting something out of every class ... are varied, like workshop-type things.... Every day [one of my teachers] would [do] different types of exercises with the work.... getting involved in activities ... actually engaging in the classroom, you know, is a huge help.

Whether they are engaging in group work, role-plays, simulations, or working on other kinds of in-class exercises, students notice how much more they absorb when they are acting like lawyers in class.

> [A] thing that has really worked well for me and for other students is the problem method ... boy, is that helpful to kind of narrow the field down ... trying to figure out what it is

you're supposed to glean from this particular subject matter.
[R]ole plays do help out a lot because … it really gets it in-
grained in your head because you're actively participating in
things.

While such activities may limit the material we can expose our students to, our students' engagement during the activities will produce deeper understanding and what they learn will be far more memorable later. For suggestions on teaching techniques, refer to Chapters 3, 4, 6, 7, and 8.

Give Students an Organizational Structure—Provide Context for Learning

Students appreciate having a detailed syllabus and learning how a particular class fits into the course as a whole. In addition, previewing the class goals and materials at the beginning of class and summarizing them at the end help students stay on track and focus their learning.

[The teacher] gave roadmaps, what she described as the best
way to understand the material. She would basically outline
on the blackboard what it was that we were going to be
doing in the next month and that gave us a very clear picture
of what was expected, of what we were going to encounter,
and it really summed up the material very well.

Make Class Preparation Assignments Reasonable and Meaningful

[W]hen you spend 3 or 4 hours preparing 25 pages of case-
book material and the professor does not mention more than
3 of those pages in the entire hour … it doesn't really encour-
age you to spend as much time and effort in preparing.

Assign students a manageable amount of reading—figure out how long it takes you to do the reading and expect that it will take students longer. If you assign reading assignments of more than 40 pages, you may want to provide suggestions about how to approach the material. Consider assigning problems or hypotheticals in addition to cases and materials.

> *[I]t would be far more productive to have small exercises that students can go and prepare for at home and then be engaged with other students. [I]f you gauge it back to 40 pages ... you can have more discussion and people will pick it up and then you can move on quicker than if you just did the 100 [pages] and everybody's crazy confused and asking fifty-million questions.*

For more suggestions about making reasonable assignments, consult Chapter 4.

Provide Opportunities for Students to Work with Others

> *Working in small groups facilitated discussion not possible in larger groups, and let all of us truly express ourselves without fear of being wrong or sounding dumb.*

Many students prefer to learn difficult material by working with others rather than in isolation. They learn a lot from verbally analyzing problems together and reading and commenting upon each other's work.

> *Cooperative exercises and role playing exercises are very useful.... [A]t some point you're going to end up arguing and even if it's simply mediation ... those are practical models of what you will have to do.*

Students appreciate being able to work with their classmates. When structured effectively, even the most introverted, small-group-work-resistant students realize the power of learning with and from their peers.

Be Aware of Students' Concerns about the Socratic Method

[T]he professors would ask questions and I would sit there and go what in the world are they asking? … I had no idea what they wanted.

The Socratic method—engaging in a dialogue with students— can be effective or ineffective. Students who like the Socratic method value having to be prepared because they may be called upon, appreciate the opportunity to practice articulating arguments and responding to questions, and enjoy hearing from a greater range of classmates. Critics note how intimidating the Socratic method can be, how disruptive it is for those who learn from listening and writing rather than talking, and how it does not engage most of the class.

[P]rofessors that are good with the Socratic method … blend in some enthusiasm that keeps you awake, and at the end of each point they clarify, well, that's not correct, or that's a good argument, but there's also this argument.

Students Want to Become Good Lawyers

The vast majority of our students plan to practice law and want to be good at it. They are eager to learn how our classes relate to their future careers. In their quest to become lawyers, students urge us to be clear about what we expect from them, offer opportunities to practice doing what we will be evaluating them on, provide feedback to help them improve, and allow multiple opportunities for them to show their progress in becoming good lawyers.

Connect What Students Are Learning to the Practice of Law

[M]y best experiences ... have been where professors actually gave you concrete examples of what is used in the real world ... actual trial transcripts ... or motions, things that we can put our hands on and say, "Okay, I understand what I'm doing now. I understand what we just spent the last month doing. I can see why we're doing this."

Students are eager to hear about how our course connects to practice. For many of them, making direct connections to practice helps the law come alive.

I was in a firm with four people; two people would be attorneys, one would be one of our witnesses.... And we actually would really get involved, really figure out what exactly it is that we need to do, that we're going to have to once we get out of this place.... [T]hat class brought back my enthusiasm for wanting to go out and practice.... I want to sit here and practice law, and that's exactly what I was doing.

Most of our students want to know how the material we teach relates to their future careers. We help students by giving them opportunities to connect class material to practice.

Be Explicit—Tell Students What You Expect and Give Them Opportunities to Practice

I think that an awful lot of times the professors start teaching a course without really knowing what they want the student to know at the end of the course.

Students want to know how they can do well in our courses; that information helps them focus their studies on the knowledge, skills, and values we want them to learn. Because our expectations are usually complex, it helps if we put our expectations in writing.

> *[Teachers]should tell us what they want … [Y]ou find out after you get your test back … [a]nd that's kind of too late.*

Students note the discrepancy between what happens in class and how they earn their grades and appreciate when the two are congruent.

> *One of the most effective ways for me to prepare for my examinations … was my professor brought in a fact pattern and we sat there in class and we worked through it. And that addresses issue spotting, brings up other sections to the pertinent law or cases.*
>
> *[T]he classes where I think you take the most away from are where you have application … although it does matter what grade you get … the grade wasn't as important because I felt that I had learned something in that course.*

Give Students Feedback on Their Progress

> *[F]eedback is absolutely critical and a lot of professors totally neglect it.… [Y]ou take exams or you write papers and some professors don't put comments on anything. And even if you've done well and there are no comments, it's impossible to learn how to do better or what, I mean, there had to have been shortcomings in your work at some point.*

As novices, students struggle to accurately self-assess their learning. They want to know, "Am I getting it?" "Should I be trying new learning strategies?"

> *[The teacher] gave us a couple of hypotheticals to turn in. She didn't grade them but she commented upon them and that was very helpful.*

Having opportunities to practice and get feedback is amazingly powerful for many students. As one student stated after being shown how to write an exam,

> *It was incredible. I felt calm. I felt powerful. I felt competent. I felt like yes, you can be a lawyer.*

And when students don't do so well, we can still provide them with positive reinforcement about their potential as lawyers.

> *[O]ne of the things that I think professors can emphasize ... success in law isn't defined only by your grades in law school, that people go on to do wonderful things ... are employed and are happy, even though they weren't in the top 10% of their class.*

Allow Students to Show Their Progress in Multiple Ways

Most students do not want their grade based solely on a course's final exam.

> *[T]he best classes that I've had have been ... [where] the professors have them do different types of assignments for a grade.... [T]he more chances ... that you can give students is better, because some students are great orally, some students are great on paper, some students do really well with multiple choice.*

Students' perspectives echo the experts': evaluating student performance on one graded event is not educationally sound. For more on evaluating students, refer to Chapter 9.

Parting Shots— Students' General Advice to Us

> *[R]epeat things, slow down a little bit ... [you] forget sometimes that we're just learning this stuff for the first time.*
> *[F]eel free to be yourself, to take chances, take risks, and to have fun because ... that's when the learning begins.*

And perhaps the best advice: *Listen. Listen. That's all.*

How to Hear *Your* Students' Perspectives

We encourage you to seek your students' views midway through each course. For suggestions on how you can gather and include students' perspectives, see Chapter 8.

Checklist for Considering the Students' Perspectives

Illustration 2-1 is a checklist you can use as you consider students' perspectives.

Illustration 2-1. Considering the Students' Perspectives Checklist

❏ **Students want to be treated with respect**
  ❏ Use students' names
  ❏ Treat students as colleagues
  ❏ Include different perspectives in class
  ❏ Create a positive and welcoming environment

❏ **Students want to be engaged in their learning**
  ❏ Use a variety of teaching methods and provide ways for students to be actively involved
  ❏ Give students an organizational structure
  ❏ Make assignments reasonable
  ❏ Allow students to work with others
  ❏ Be aware of problems with the Socratic method

❏ **Students want to become good lawyers**
  ❏ Connect learning to law practice
  ❏ Be explicit about what you expect
  ❏ Give students opportunities to practice
  ❏ Give feedback
  ❏ Allow students to show progress in multiple ways

Chapter 3

Designing the Course

Introduction

Chapter 3 marks a transition in this book. Chapters 1 and 2 focused on theory and on understanding law students; this chapter and all of those that follow translate years of research on effective teaching into a set of concrete suggestions.

In this chapter, we offer ideas for designing courses. Most broadly, course design is a recursive process, as reflected in Illustration 3-1, in which you: (1) identify the skills, knowledge, and values you want your students to learn ("set course goals"); (2) evaluate your students' incoming knowledge, skills, and values ("assess the learners"); (3) decide how you will assess (a) whether students have attained the course goals and (b) whether your course design decisions are good ones, and then (c) design appropriate assessments ("plan assessment"); (4) select texts; (5) design the course to help the students achieve the course goals, which includes writing the syllabus ("design the course"); (6) design a course webpage ("create course web")—if you are going to do so; (7) implement the design; (8) evaluate the course design; and, finally, (9) using the information you gained from evaluating the course, redesign the course according to the same process.

We have organized the rest of this chapter according to the timeline suggested by Illustration 3-1.

Illustration 3-1. The Recursive Course Design Process

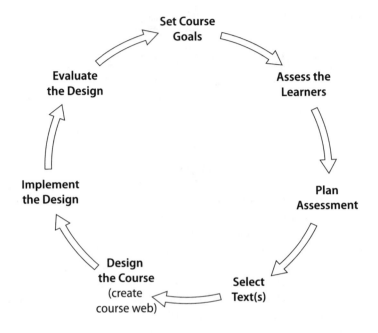

Initiating the Design Process: Setting Course Goals

A goal is a statement of what students should be able to do by the end of your course. Goals influence which topics you teach, what you expect of your students, and how you design your syllabus, class sessions, examinations, and paper assignments.

A good place to start in identifying goals is thinking about what you can do in this field *because* you are an expert. Another way is to imagine your students a few years after they have taken your course. What do you hope the students have retained from the course? We encourage you to be ambitious in describing your course goals—think beyond the limits of your assigned course label (e.g., pre-trial practice, environmental law). Aspire to produce learning that transcends. Limit yourself to three or four learning goals per course, and focus not on what students should know but, rather, what they should be able to do.

All courses involve a mix of higher-level goals and lower-level thinking skills. In the law school context, higher-level skills include: drafting law-related documents, analyzing and solving legal problems, evaluating cases, conducting client and witness interviews, etc. These higher-level skills implicate lower level skills such as finding, understanding, and being able to explain the applicable law.

One final thought about goals: as an adjunct faculty member you bring some things to the classroom that full-time teachers often cannot—a practical, real-world perspective. Rather than setting academic goals, consider setting goals that relate to what you uniquely offer your students.

Know Your Students:
Assessing the Learners

The most common error committed by law professors is assuming their students are like them. In fact, recent studies suggest law professors are more like each other and much less like their students, particularly in terms of the characteristics that might influence designing a law school course. This difference between law professors and students is exacerbated because our own law school experiences were several years ago. Law professors also often have different learning style preferences than their students. Unlike most law professors, many law students enjoy learning through collaboration with others and prefer visually-focused learning experiences. Of course, law students also tend to vary among themselves in their learning preferences. In short, we cannot assume that our students will best learn law the way we did.

Plan Assessment:
How Will You Know Whether Your
Students Are Learning?

Thinking about assessment before you start designing your course may seem counter-intuitive. You may even worry that, if you were to design assessment instruments before you designed your course, you might end up "teaching to the test." Designing your assessment instruments right after you have articulated your objectives and before you design your course ensures that your assessment instruments are congruent with your course goals, a hallmark of a fair and well-designed course.

In fact, the process of designing assessment instruments may cause you to revise your course goals; in other words, your assessment instruments may reveal to you what you really believe is critical learning in your course. Even more significantly, designing your assessment instruments and revising your goals will (and should) influence how you design your course. Your assessment instruments should focus on assessing student learning of the skills you regard as most important, and you should be designing your course so that you and your students devote the greatest amount of time and effort to developing those skills.

Finding the Book of Your Dreams:
Sifting the Morass to Find the
Right Textbook for You

Start by surveying others who teach your subject or ask a colleague, but, as tempting as it is to follow the majority, we suggest you dig deeper. *The core principle in selecting a textbook is finding the book that best furthers as many of your course goals as possible without undermining any of your other course goals.* A good textbook for you is one that makes it easier for you to help your students develop the skills, knowledge and values you hope to teach them. Illustration 3-2 is a tool to help you consider the most significant textbook selection considerations.

Illustration 3-2. Textbook Evaluation Tool

Author(s) Title Publisher	Congruence with Your Objectives	Case Selection and Sequencing	Quality and Quantity of Problems	Quality and Quantity of Questions	Teacher's Manual: Assessment Help	Teacher's Manual: Teaching Help
Text #1:						
Text #2:						
Text #3:						

Designing the Course So Students Will Learn What You Want Them to Learn

This discussion focuses on the guiding principles of course design. As you consider these suggestions in the light of your own course planning efforts, keep your list of learning goals and assessments by your side. As the discussion below reflects, the learning goals and assessments will guide your course design decisions.

Start by dividing your overall learning goals into at least five and as many as eight or nine sub-categories, called "learning units." Be careful not to allow coverage of every topic in your field to be the single driving factor in your course design. Students will forget large chunks of the doctrine soon after your final exam. While we encourage you to develop a list of doctrinal categories, we discourage you from limiting your sub-category list to doctrine. If your course goals include developing your students' ability to engage in problem-solving in your field, you need to prioritize teaching time for this skill.

The most valuable thing you can provide to students is practice and feedback. New learners in a field need learning experiences that allow them to practice applying each of the concepts and principles in isolation *and* they need instruction and practice in combing those concepts and principles and procedures to analyze complex problems that implicate multiple doctrinal areas. In other words, your casebook may need supplementation. You may need to provide students with readings and other materials specifically directed to the problem-solving tasks in which they will be engaging (e.g., readings on conducting client interviews or drafting pleadings, will, trusts, or contracts).

In terms of class preparation assignments, the research strongly suggests that students learn more and learn it better when they read cases for the purpose of solving a problem, and students are more likely to give skills reading assignments the required attention if those assignments are situated in a simulated law practice problem. The research also suggests law students learn more from cases when they possess relevant prior knowledge *before* they begin reading. Consequently, consider providing or assigning introductory readings.

Moreover, students learn more when they engage in deep processing of the materials. By expanding your conception of the term "assignments" and therefore explicitly assigning tasks in addition to reading a list of assigned cases and statutes, you can engage your students in a wide spectrum of intellectually-challenging learning activities, including:

- developing a theory that explains the need for the doctrine;
- synthesizing the reading assignments with past assignments;
- comparing a case or series of cases to an existing or proposed statute;
- developing examples and non-examples of a concept addressed in their readings;
- analyzing hypotheticals;
- generating hypothetical problems;
- drafting a pleading or contract clause designed to address the problem; or
- drafting a proposed statute to address a problem raised by a line of cases.

Thinking through the kinds of activities in which you want your students to engage is crucial because you want to be sure that you maximize your classroom time with students. Educational experts frequently talk in terms of selecting the best medium for delivering a particular aspect of students' learning. Available instructional media include: texts, live teachers, computer programs, websites, videotapes, podcasts, and small group experiences. Live teachers, in comparison to all alternative media of instruction, are uniquely flexible and adaptable and uniquely possess empathy. Live teachers can be the best instructional medium for inspiring learners, and we possess the unique ability to teach by functioning as role models. Consequently, you need to be making conscious decisions about what aspects of your teaching require your physical presence and what aspects can be moved to another instructional medium.

Having decided how you will structure each individual learning unit, you are ready to consider how you will combine the units to design your course. As you begin this synthesis process, keep the following considerations in mind.

First, consider how best to sequence your learning units and, within each learning unit, consider how best to sequence students' progress through that unit. Don't assume the author of your casebook knows best. Students prosper when their learning experiences are challenging but not overwhelming and when the professor gradually increases the difficulty of the intellectual challenge in the course. Sequencing also is a matter of prioritizing. Many of us teach our courses as if the most important topics are the ones with which we start and the least important are those at the end. In fact, the opposite may be true. And students learn little when, in an effort to "finish" our syllabus, we abandon all semblance of active engagement, use lecture format all the time, and move through the materials like tanks through wet paper.

Second, consider the burden you are imposing on the students, their competing obligations in other courses, and the importance of school-life balance for your students.

Third, make sure you consciously sequence your course for variety. Variety allows us to retain our students' attention and cater to every student's learning preference. For example, your law practice problems should engage students in the wide spectrum of activities in which lawyers engage, including arguing, evaluating, reading, drafting, re-writing, negotiating, communicating with others (clients, colleagues, other lawyers, judges), interviewing, planning, and presenting.

Finally, carefully plan how you will begin and end your course. Beginnings should help students see what is exciting about your course. Endings should provide students with opportunities to reflect on what they have learned and consider how they will use it.

Writing Your Syllabus

Your syllabus can be just a list of assignments. But it also can be culture-making. In many instances, our first interaction with our students occurs via the course syllabus. Our syllabi can engage students, inspire their confidence and interest in you and your subject, communicate your investment in their success, display your professionalism as a teacher, demonstrate your skill in planning the course, and establish high expectations. Your syllabus also can leave students cold or, worse yet, discouraged, disinterested, disengaged, anxious, confused, and hostile.

Syllabus construction is mostly a matter of science and careful decision-making, but it is also art. The science suggests you should address certain topics in your syllabus and follow best practices in addressing those topics. At the same time, your syllabus communicates a lot about you: based on your syllabus, your students will draw inferences about who you are and how you will teach.

Your syllabus serves as a contract between you and the students. It defines your relationship, establishes your respective rights, and creates your respective responsibilities. As with any contract, problems arise if the obligations it describes are ambiguous or if either party asserts rules or expectations not articulated in the writing. Consequently, make sure you have a colleague read your syllabus before you distribute it to students.

Syllabi should provide the basic information students need and should address all the issues that reasonably might arise in the class, including:

- your name and contact information, your office hours, and how to schedule appointments;
- the name of the course, the required texts, and a description of the course;
- your expectations in terms of attendance and timely arrival for class;
- your course goals, your teaching philosophy, and your teaching methods;
- your expectations for class preparation and other classroom conduct;
- a schedule of class meetings, readings, projects, and other assignments;
- your policies for grading, late assignments, and failures to complete assigned projects; and
- your rules relating to plagiarism and/or any other forms of academic misconduct that may arise in your class.

If you have a course webpage, your syllabus should provide information about accessing it and your policies for using it. (Some institutions mandate the inclusion of certain additional information in syllabi, such as the institution's mission statement, information about disability accommodations, and other such matters. Check with your institution.)

Consider also the degree to which you wish to give yourself leeway to modify the policies stated in your syllabus. If you wish to retain the ability to modify your course policies or assignments, be sure your syllabus communicates that you can do so. You either can have a general caveat explaining that the syllabus is subject to change or specifically address areas where change is a genuine possibility. For example, if you wish to retain the right to modify your final exam format, you can say, "The format of the final exam is subject to change."

For many students, the schedule of class assignments and the grading policies are the only sections they carefully read.

Students want specific details about when and how the professor expects them to fulfill their scholastic duties. Your schedule should include all assignments and projects, the dates they are due, and the dates of any exams. Organize these elements by topic rather than by chapter or page numbers. Clarity is crucial. A clear course road map provides each student an opportunity to formulate a "plan of attack" that compliments his or her learning preferences. At the same time, both students and professors prefer the professor retain some discretion to modify the assignments after the semester begins. An easy way to retain this flexibility is by including a disclaimer at the beginning of this section of your syllabus that states "To maximize student learning in this class, I may need to adjust the assignments. I promise to give you at least one week's notice before implementing any such change."

Students also need and deserve to know what weight will be placed on the various graded activities in the course and whether other factors such as class participation and course webpage contributions will be factored into their grades. It is particularly useful to provide students with guidance about the standards by which you will be evaluating their work. Such grading rubrics (see Chapter 7 for additional information) help eliminate confusion and concerns over the accuracy or fairness of grading. If your students will be handing in work, make sure you also communicate policies addressing what happens if students hand in assignments late or not at all.

Finally, before you start writing any of the sections, think carefully about the overarching messages you wish to communicate to your students. Students will draw inferences about who you are, what you value, what you think of your students, and how you will teach based solely on what you say in your syllabus and the tone with which you say it. For example, you may find it helpful to include some self-deprecating humor in your syllabus. Many law students experience law professors as arrogant. You also should ask a lot of your students, communicate confidence in your ability to teach, and express confidence in your students' ability to learn. Because teacher enthusiasm facilitates student learning, your syllabus should express enthusiasm for your subject.

Because law students are adult learners (for the most part), one of the best things you can do to enhance their learning experience is to share your power to establish course policies. By ceding some power to students, you convey important messages about your sense of the students' competence, autonomy, and abilities. You also show that you have faith in and respect for them and that you have confidence in your own ability to synthesize their needs and the course goals. The easiest facet of your syllabus for sharing control is course coverage. Select those topics you regard as essential and then let your students select from among the remaining topics. All three of us also have found it easy to allow students to articulate their expectations of us and to suggest teaching methods they would like us to include in our repertoire. You can also ask students to develop or contribute to your list of student expectations and for input into your grading scheme.

Evaluate the Design and Plan for the Future

Having designed the course, created a syllabus and set up a course webpage, the next logical step, of course, would be to implement, i.e., teach, the course. If you have adopted the recommendations of this book, your course design has embedded multiple assessments so that throughout the semester, you are gathering data about how well your students are learning and, where possible, adjusting the design of your course.

Ideally, the goal in course evaluation and redesign is to be systematic, reflective and continuous. Your approach is systematic to the extent that the information you strive to develop from your efforts at assessing your students' learning covers the breadth and depth of skills, knowledge and values you teach and evaluates student learning of all learning objectives. Your evaluation process is reflective if you devote time and effort to reflecting (in a teaching journal for example) on each class session and on the results of your efforts at assessment. Finally, the word "continuous" conveys the idea that your efforts should continue throughout the semester and with respect to each offering of your course. The idea is analogous to the continuous improvement model in business planning. In both contexts, data is used to inform future planning and each implementation is treated as an opportunity to improve.

Checklist for Course Design Process

Illustration 3-3 is a checklist you can use as you work through the course design process.

Illustration 3-3. Course Design Process Checklist

❏ Determine what you want students to know, value, and be able to do

❏ Figure out who your students are

❏ Decide how you will assess students and draft assessments

❏ Choose texts

❏ Design each part of the course

❏ Design the course as a whole

❏ Create a syllabus that
  ❏ provides the basic information students need and addresses all the issues that reasonably might arise in the class
  ❏ engages students
  ❏ communicates high expectations
  ❏ includes challenging and appropriate reading and problem-solving assignments
  ❏ paces the course carefully to make sure the course has an engaging opening and an effective closing and avoids the end-of-semester rush
  ❏ devotes instructional time to problem-solving instruction and experiences

❏ Create a course webpage (if you have decided to have one)

❏ Implement your design

❏ Evaluate your design

You will find examples of the concepts from this chapter in Appendix 3 on the book's website—http://lawteaching.org/resources.

Appendix 3-1: Course Goals

Appendix 3-2: Lesson Objectives

Appendix 3-3: Syllabi

Chapter 4

Designing Each Class Session

Law school class sessions can lead to significant student learning and teacher satisfaction if you adopt an intentional approach to class design. We recommend a five-step class design process, reflected in Illustration 4-1. We recognize that this process is more elaborate than most law teachers' class planning, but many teachers implicitly engage in much of the process. Even if the entire process is not for you, you can improve your teaching and your students' learning by expanding your class design efforts in any of the elements described below.

Illustration 4-1. Five-Step Class Design Process

Context

Each class occurs in a larger context, which includes important background aspects of the course, the students, and the teacher. Analyzing the context should consume very little of the teacher's planning time. All we need to do is spend a few minutes thinking about the context before we move on to the rest of the class design process.

Course Context

Law schools may mandate that certain concepts or skills be taught in required courses to prepare students for subsequent courses, the bar exam, or practice. Elective courses may provide faculty members with more options. Time, scheduling and place in the course also influence class planning. Designing a class that meets for an hour three times per week in the morning should differ from a class that meets once per week for three hours at night. Where the class fits in the life of the course has a significant influence on class design as well.

Student Context

Our students' needs and motivation change as they progress through law school. Most first-semester, first-year students are interested in their courses and eager to learn. Second and third-year law students may display less interest in their courses but are eager to graduate, pass the bar exam, and begin their careers. They may respond well to a class with content and skills that are directly relevant to law practice, such as preparing a will. Similarly, students' previous exposure to the material will affect class design, as will their real world experience with the subject. In addition, the numbers of students affects course design.

A variety of active learning methods and feedback are essential elements of successful class sessions regardless of the size of the class. Nevertheless, enrollment affects the objectives, instructional activities, material, and feedback for a class.

Teacher Context

We all have strengths and weaknesses as teachers. We are more comfortable with some teaching methods, content, and skills than others. In designing classes, we should build on our strengths and address our weaknesses. Classes that address content and skills with which we are comfortable may be appropriate to experiment with new learning and feedback activities. On days when we are on shakier ground or are struggling with other matters, we may choose to stick with the tried and true.

Class Objectives

Objectives are the foundation on which each class should be built. The number of objectives appropriate for a single class session depends on all of the context issues above. In general, we favor depth over breadth and significant learning over coverage. Consequently, one to three class objectives are generally appropriate for a one-hour class session.

The objectives for each class should have three basic characteristics. They should:

- Be learner, rather than teacher, centered;
- Encompass a broad range of professional knowledge, skills, and values; and
- Be clear and concrete.

Learner Centered

Learner-centered objectives focus on what students will learn, rather than what the teacher will do or cover in class. To focus on student learning, begin class objectives with the phrase "As a result of this class, students will be able to." Then, complete each objective with the knowledge, skills, or values that students should learn in the class session. For example, rather than having the class objective be to get through 20 pages of material, cover three cases, discuss four problems, present an analytical framework or demonstrate a skill, your class objective could be: "As a result of this class, students will be able to use six components of statutory interpretation to analyze problems involving statutes and regulations."

Professional Knowledge, Skills, and Values

Because success as a lawyer rests on a set of knowledge, skills, and values, class objectives should focus on students learning and practicing knowledge, skills, and values related to the course. As we design a class session, we should focus on the critical knowledge, skills, or values. Choosing and articulating class objectives helps us make those choices intentionally.

For most law school courses, knowledge includes legal doctrine, policy, and theory. An individual class session will focus on a small subset of the relevant knowledge for the course. Many courses also address thinking skills, including case analysis, statutory analysis, problem solving, or critical thinking. In addition, we should include other skills lawyers need to succeed in practice. For example, one well-respected report lists ten "Fundamental Lawyering Skills": problem solving, legal analysis and reasoning, legal research, fact investigations, oral and written communication, counseling, negotiation, litigation and alternative dispute resolution, organization and management of legal work, and recognizing and resolving ethical dilemmas. Professional attributes and values are perhaps the most overlooked aspect of traditional legal education. Yet lawyers consistently identify a number of aspects of professionalism as important to success in law practice, including honesty, integrity, reliability, responsibility, judgment, diligence, tolerance, self-motivation, empathy, and respect for clients, lawyers, judges, and staff. We should look for opportunities to include values in our class objectives.

Clear and Concrete

The key to clear and concrete class objectives is to focus on observable student behavior. We can't observe students "understanding" a concept or "appreciating" a value. We can observe students laying out the analytical framework for an area of law, identifying legal issues in a fact pattern, or demonstrating respect for other students in the classroom.

Although we believe deeply in the importance of articulating class objectives, we believe their form is flexible. Our class objectives are the answers to: "What are the few 'essentials' in terms of knowledge, skills, or values that the students should have when they leave this class session?" Those answers should drive our design of instructional activities, feedback, and materials.

Instructional Activities

Effective class planning requires designing what we will do during the class and what our students will do. For design purposes, we divide the instructional activities in class into three sections: (1) opening—the first one to five minutes; (2) body—the bulk of the class period; and (3) closing—the final one to five minutes.

Opening

The first few minutes of a class can be the most valuable. Our opening can grab attention, motivate, communicate objectives, and build a bridge to previous learning. We can plan to gain students' attention in many different ways—a projected image relevant to the subject for that day, a mental challenge represented by an overarching question for the lesson, a news story, or by celebrating student success. Once we have students' attention, we should motivate them to engage by communicating our own passion for the subject or by showing students how the concepts or skills for the class will be relevant and valuable to them in their personal lives, on the bar exam, or in practice.

Share class objectives with the students to focus student learning. When students know what they need to be learning, they can devote their effort to the essentials, rather than tangential matters. Finally, plan the transition from previous classes. Put the day's class in the larger context of the course. Help students see the big picture by using a diagram or example to show them how to fit the lesson into the rest of the course.

Body

The primary design decision for the body of the class is selecting teaching and learning methods. Use one overarching principle— choose methods to maximize student learning of class objectives. Teaching and learning methods such as Socratic dialogue, lecture, or simulations are not "good" or "bad" methods. They are tools to facilitate student learning and their appropriateness varies according to class objectives.

Two subsidiary considerations are relevant to our choice of teaching and learning methods—learning style preferences and depth of learning. Below, we summarize and apply Fleming and Mills' sensory-based learning style model, which identifies four learning style preferences. Illustration 4-2 identifies the four styles and examples of teaching learning methods that are most comfortable for each style.

Illustration 4-2. Sensory Based Learning Styles

Learning Style	Teaching/Learning Methods
Digital • Learn via reading and writing • Logical, deductive reasoning • Abstract thinkers • Find patterns and organization	• Read to prepare for class • Brief cases • Write responses to problems • Outline course • Lecture—listen and take notes
Auditory • Learn via hearing and speaking • Process and store information chronologically • Memory aided by mnemonic devices	• Socratic dialogue • Large group discussion • Small group problem solving • Debate • Listen to stories, cases, hypotheticals
Visual • Learn via sight • Organize concepts through spatial relationships • Store ideas graphically	• Visual tools of all types— whiteboard, pictures, videos, handouts, slides • Diagrams, flow charts, graphs, concept maps
Kinesthetic • Learn by doing • Store knowledge as experience • Attend to physical and emotional manifestation of concepts	• Simulations and role plays • Authentic law practice experiences, including service learning, clinical, and externship experiences • Real documents—pleadings, contracts, deeds

The learning styles literature does not suggest we plan methods to address each learning style preference in each class. But because students prefer to learn in various ways, we should plan to use more than one method for each class session and should incorporate many methods over the life of the course. In fact, evidence suggests that all students benefit from learning in ways with which they are less comfortable. This conclusion is bolstered by empirical research on the effect on learning of multiple-sense, multiple-method instruction. In general students learn more when instruction accesses multiple senses—seeing, hearing, speaking, doing.

In every course, some content and skills are more important than others. We should design instructional activities that involve multiple senses and methods for the most important aspects of the course. For example, if a significant learning objective is for students to be able to apply the law, policy, and strategy involved in creating security agreements, we may ask students to read applicable sections of the Uniform Commercial Code, discuss cases or problems applying those sections, review a sample security agreement, and draft a security agreement for a hypothetical or real client.

Closing

The last few minutes of class can include significant learning. We can plan the last few minutes of class to review, summarize, transfer learning, provide feedback, conduct classroom assessment, and re-motivate students.

Students need to consolidate new learning. We can review and comment briefly on the class objectives or articulate the few essential concepts, skills, or values students should have grasped in the class. With a graphic projected on a screen or with a handout, we could demonstrate how the doctrine, theory, or skills fit in the larger scheme or analytical framework. Students can play an active role in the closing by voicing the key concepts they learned in that class or by completing a diagram or chart that draws together the learning for that day. We can facilitate transfer of learning and re-motivate students by showing how the knowledge, skills, and values learned during a class will be valuable in the remainder of the course, on the bar exam, or in the profession after graduation.

Feedback

Feedback is crucial to effective teaching and learning and should be a part of our course design, class planning, and the teaching/learning activities we use with our students. As we design class sessions, we should look for ways to incorporate formative feedback, designed to help students improve. By the end of the course, feedback should have been part of many class sessions, having occurred at various points in a class session.

- **Opening.** Feedback is an excellent way to gain students' attention and to build a bridge to prior learning. Class could begin with a short multiple-choice quiz that addresses key concepts from a prior classes and important aspects of the current class. The quiz could be on a handout, a slide, or with a "clicker" system. Immediate feedback should follow the quiz.
- **Body.** During the bulk of the class period, feedback can vary from simple to elaborate. For example, when a student performs a skill well, we can call attention to it briefly—"Jan just synthesized a line of cases by ..." or "Frank drafted an excellent set of interrogatories that...." Or we could spend half of a class period going over the rubric or score sheet for a practice exam and involving students in assessing their exam performance.
- **Closing.** By reviewing the class objectives or summarizing the major points for the class (done either by the teacher or students), the students get feedback on the critical content, skills, and values they should have learned that day. Or the class could end with a problem that integrates the learning for that day—feedback on the appropriate analysis could be immediate, happen via the course web page, or be part of the opening of the next class.
- **After class.** Feedback on quizzes, problems, hypotheticals, outlines, etc. can take place in a discussion on the course web page, via an applicable CALI exercise, or one-on-one in the teacher's office. We believe that a primary obligation of effective teachers is to provide feedback to students. For more on feedback and assessment, see Chapter 9.

Materials

Materials include both print and electronic resources that students will use outside of class or that students and teachers will use during class. Examples include readings, websites, pictures, videos, computer exercises, handouts, slides, objects, and items written on the board.

We can choose and design materials to achieve our objectives, guide student preparation, support other instructional activities, and facilitate feedback. These four functions of materials provide guidance on the types of materials we should select for each class. Different class objectives, instructional activities, and feedback call for different types of materials. Several additional considerations apply regardless of the type of material. Effective materials are selective, variable, focused, and interactive.

Selective. For virtually any topic we address in class, we could find thousands of pages of text (cases, statutes, articles) along with websites, pictures, and videos. Consequently, for every class session, we are choosing a tiny slice of the available material. What should guide those choices? First, we should select the material that is most relevant to our class objectives. Second, we should limit the material we assign to students to a reasonable amount. We believe that two hours of student preparation for each hour of class is reasonable. Selectivity applies to our use of materials during class as well. Research shows that students will copy verbatim anything we write on the board or project on a screen. A few key phrases or a clear, simple flow chart will aid student learning more than a board covered with our writing or slides jammed with text.

Variable. Variety in materials is a virtue for several reasons. In modern life, we get information from both print and electronic sources. Our class materials should reflect that reality. We miss opportunities to enhance our students' learning if we march through the casebook without incorporating relevant stories, documents, and images. Further, variety makes our classes more interesting. Each time we shift material in the classroom, we grab attention.

Focused. One way to facilitate student preparation for class is to provide questions about the material before class. These questions allow students to focus their preparation, just as a lawyer prepares for the issues that will be central to a motion hearing. We ask many other questions in class as well, just as judges ask lawyers questions in court. We can provide the advance questions to students in writing via a supplement, webpage, email, or a handout. Focus questions can address doctrine, skills, and values. We can use focus devices in material we prepare to use in class. For example, we can focus student's attention in handouts and on slides through text boxes, bullets, numbering, font, symbols, or color.

Interactive. Much of the material we assign to students is designed for students to read, such as cases, statutes, and articles. Likewise, materials we use in class are often intended for students to read or view, including slides, handouts, pictures, and diagrams. This type of material is valuable for presenting doctrine, policy, analytical frameworks, and theory to students. To maximize the effectiveness of material in achieving class objectives, we should look for ways to make materials interactive as well.

Simple techniques can add interactive features to many types of materials.

- **Readings.** The most passive use of readings is to simply assign pages. We can encourage more active reading by giving students focus questions (discussed above) or by asking students to do something with the reading—brief a case, apply a statute to a problem, or synthesize the law and policy from the material.
- **Videos.** Short video clips relevant to the class objectives can be powerful instructional tools. We can record our own short videos or find video clips on line. Books such as *Reel Justice* describe portions of movies that illustrate doctrine, skills, and values. We can make the clips even more effective by providing students with questions or problems to focus their attention.
- **Slides.** Presentation software, such as PowerPoint, allows us to produce slides that transmit information and images to students. These visual aids are helpful to many students. However, if we use slides extensively and the slides do no more than present information, many students will become passive re-

ceivers. We can change this dynamic by including slides with questions, problems, quizzes, and hypotheticals designed to facilitate active student engagement in the classroom.

- **Boards, flip charts, and projectors.** These basic tools excel at supporting discussions. We can easily capture student contributions to class discussions on the board, a chart, or a document projector.
- **Word processing software.** We can accomplish the interactive aspects of presentation software and boards by projecting a document on a screen in word processing software.
- **Diagrams, flow charts, and tables.** These tools can be excellent devices to organize concepts and illustrate the interrelationships among ideas. Better yet, we can provide students with partially completed or blank diagrams and tables and have students complete them before or during class.
- **Handouts.** We can accomplish many of the functions of materials with handouts, distributed in either paper or electronic form. The interactivity of a handout we design for use during class depends in part on how we incorporate white space. Studies compared the learning results of (1) students given the professor's notes, (2) students given a barebones outline into which they can take notes, and (3) students given nothing. The students in group (2) learned the most and the students in group (1) and (3) learned at about the same level.

Evaluate and Revise

We encourage you to engage in a systematic, reflective, continuous process for evaluating and revising class designs. After class, spend five minutes reflecting. Were the class objectives achieved? How effective were the opening and closing? Which teaching and learning activities were most and least effective? Did you provide feedback to students? Were the materials appropriate and effective? Memorialize your reflections in writing and keep them someplace that you will not lose them, such as with your notes for the class or in a teaching log.

The next time you teach the class, begin your preparation by reviewing your reflections. Then, after considering the new context that will apply the next time you teach the class, make appropriate revisions in the objectives, instructional activities, feedback devices, and materials.

There is no such thing as a perfect class session and we do not seek perfection in our classes. Instead, we strive to make incremental improvements in our classes over time. The class design process helps improve teaching and enhance students' learning class-by-class.

Checklist for Class Design Process

Illustration 4-3 is a checklist you can use as you work through the class design process.

Illustration 4-3. Class Design Process Checklist

❑ **Consider the context of the class**
    ❑ Course context
    ❑ Student context
    ❑ Teacher context

❑ **Draft learner-centered, clear, concrete class objectives**
    ❑ Knowledge (doctrine, theory)
    ❑ Professional skills (thinking, performance)
    ❑ Professional values

❑ **Choose instructional activities to achieve class goals**
    ❑ Opening
    ❑ Body (teaching/learning activities)
    ❑ Closing

❑ **Provide feedback to students**

❑ **Select materials**
    ❑ Use outside class (readings, CALI, Internet)
    ❑ Use in class (slides, whiteboard, videos, diagrams, handouts)

❑ **Evaluate your design**

You will find examples of the concepts from this chapter in Appendix 4 on the book's website—http://lawteaching.org/resources.

Appendix 4-1: Charts, Tables, and Diagrams
 Dismissal under FRCP 41 Chart
 Chart Depicting Restitution in the Context of a
  Contracts Course
 Common Contract Terms Chart
 Personal Jurisdiction Analytical Framework
 Partially Completed Graphic Organizer Synthesizing
  Contract Interpretation Principles

Chapter 5

Student Motivation, Attitudes, and Self-Regulation

Introduction

"It's easy to teach 1Ls. But how do you motivate burnt-out 3Ls?"

"One day in class, I called on three students, and none of them were prepared. I just wanted to walk right back out of the room! What else could I do?"

"I want my students to develop a sense of professionalism and a commitment to the lawyer's responsibility to serve the community. But how do you teach values?"

"My students just want to be spoon-fed. They don't want to do any of the work for themselves. How do I get my students to take control over their own learning?"

We often hear smart, dedicated law teachers express concerns about motivating their students, about changing or developing student attitudes and values, and about training law students to be self-motivated, reflective, lifelong learners. This chapter addresses these concerns from several perspectives.

Motivating Students

Introduction

Motivating students is, in many ways, a natural outgrowth of adopting the good teaching principles we describe in this book.

Educational experts often describe the purpose of motivating students as trying to increase the likelihood that students achieve the state known as "flow." In the academic context, flow refers to a mental and emotional state in which the student experiences a task as exciting and challenging yet attainable. The student feels confident yet pressed to grow, engaged yet not over-stimulated. Students who feel a sense of flow immerse themselves in the learning process. They feel less inhibited than normal and also feel in control. Even though the work may be challenging, they experience the work as effortless. In many instances, a student who experiences flow is so engaged in the learning process the student loses track of time. Most of us have had at least a few class sessions in which both we and our students have lost ourselves in the thrill of learning. Wouldn't it be great to have more such sessions? How can we systematically and reflectively teach for flow?

Experts draw an important distinction between teacher efforts fostering students' extrinsic motivation and efforts designed to help students find intrinsic motivation. Extrinsic motivation emphasizes things teachers do to reward student engagement and to impose natural consequences for student disengagement. Extrinsic motivational possibilities include emphasizing grades, administering pop quizzes, and considering class participation in students' grades.

While extrinsic factors can influence motivation, they seldom produce the long-range satisfaction and sustained interest possible when students are intrinsically motivated. In educational settings, intrinsic motivation refers to qualities and circumstances within the student or the learning activity that stimulate engagement in a course. Recent studies have focused on techniques teachers can use to stimulate the development of intrinsic student interest. These studies, taken together, prescribe a wide variety of choices for inspiring and motivating students.

Specific Techniques

Teacher Attitudes That Motivate Students

Teacher passion and confidence significantly influence student motivation. As we explain in Chapters 1, 2, 6, and 8, students frequently describe their most inspiring teachers as passionate about their subjects and about student learning and confident in themselves and in their students' ability to learn. These attitudes help students discover the excitement that led their professors to become law teachers in the first place and to feel confident in their ability to learn what we want them to learn. Teachers can show passion for student learning by expressing excitement about students' insights, by making themselves available to students, by actively and explicitly looking for new ways to help students learn, and by treating student learning as the principle goal in their classes. If a student suggests a new insight or a new way of understanding a concept or explains a difficult concept well, expressing delight in this success and acknowledging the student's influence on your thinking can provide significant motivation for students. When a teacher communicates that the students can change the teacher's thinking or approach to teaching course material, the students are more likely to be motivated to engage in the kinds of behaviors likely to produce such insights.

Law teachers can show their confidence in themselves and their students by what they choose to teach, by the particular teaching methods they adopt, by the language they use as they teach, and by how they otherwise interact with their students. For example, the choice to teach difficult materials and to ask students to solve challenging problems manifests confidence in both the teacher and the students. The students get the idea that the teacher believes the students can learn anything.

Likewise, when teachers create learning activities in which students develop their own insights and must manifest their developing expertise, such as cooperative learning exercises, peer feedback experiences, and peer-to-peer teaching, they convey their belief that the students are capable. Well-designed cooperative learning experiences show faith in students because they allow students to negotiate meaning among themselves—the students construct ideas among themselves rather than passively receiving the ideas.

Very simple things, such as our body language in class, how we react to questions in class, how we deal with student frustration, and our comfort in demonstrating our expertise while acknowledging our errors also express our confidence. For example, respectfully listening to students, and finding and reinforcing the insights embedded in students' comments, course webpage contributions, and questions show that we are convinced that the students are perceptive and have promising futures in the field.

Authentic Experiences, Variety, and Active Learning

As we also explain in Chapters 1, 2, 4, 6, 7, and 8, students learn more and learn it better when they engage in a variety of authentic lawyering experiences that involve active learning. Authentic experiences, variety, and active learning experiences also can be motivational because all three help maintain student interest in the learning process.

By situating students in their new roles as lawyers, authentic experiences explicitly connect students' new learning with their career aspirations. The concreteness of this link attracts students' interest. Students develop the motivation to learn because the connection between what they are learning and what they want to be doing is direct and the consequences of not learning seem more significant.

Variety and active learning experiences can be motivating because they capture students' attention and minimize distraction. Changes in the learning process recapture students' attention and motivate students to continue trying to learn, especially if the overall cycle of teaching methods includes techniques preferred by the students. Active learning motivates students because it prevents them from mentally withdrawing.

Structuring Student Autonomy

Student autonomy is highly correlated with student motivation. Thus, giving students power to make choices about how the class will be taught and what they will learn is particularly effective for motivating students. Disclosing learning goals, providing students with mechanisms to self-evaluate their progress, and explicitly explaining the criteria by which students will be evaluated (i.e., creating rubrics) also foster student autonomy. This information empowers students to control their own learning process.

Participation (Role-Playing)

Engaging students in role-plays can be particularly effective for motivating students. As explained above, asking students to assume their future lawyer role helps students identify the importance of what they are learning. But role-playing also can be useful for motivating students in other ways. Asking students to take the various roles involved in a transaction or dispute can motivate them to master difficult concepts by providing context with which they may not be familiar.

Challenge, Incongruity, and Conflict

Of all the techniques educators suggest as tools to motivate students to learn, incongruity and conflict is the one law professors most commonly use. The law school Socratic method focuses heavily on introducing students to considerations and ideas that either actually contradict their viewpoints or seem to do so. However, students cannot develop flow if they perceive success as unattainable. If you adopt this teaching method, make sure your students experience some success in resolving (or at least understanding) the conflicts and incongruities. Unending failure is de-motivating. Challenge works best as a motivational tool when the challenge is *both* reasonable and continuous. By sequencing course materials and learning activities so that the students' learning tasks are increasingly difficult, law teachers can make sure students get both the benefits of being challenged while also enjoying success and being reinforced for their persistence.

Reinforcement

Reinforcement also can be effective in motivating students. In general, however, reinforcement tends to focus students on extrinsic rather than intrinsic goals and therefore is less likely to persist as a motivator. Effective reinforcements include praise, public recognition, and unexpected prizes. Reinforcement also can take the form of eliminating an obstacle or hurdle that is unattractive to your students, such as allowing students to pass their way out of having to complete an exercise. In contrast, threats, surveillance practices, and punishments are less effective in stimulating motivation. These techniques tend to produce student anger, negativity and, in some instances, rebellion.

Teaching for Attitude or Value Change or Development

Law schools and teachers commonly assert that they want their students to develop the attitudes and values of professionalism, commitment to public service, sensitivity to diversity, respect for the rule of law, and belief in professional reflection and lifelong learning. The research suggests students can be taught values. As you might expect, however, simply telling students to have a value is seldom effective.

General Principles of Attitude Learning

Experts in attitude instruction focus on *evidence* of attitude change; that evidence is measured in terms of student behavior. Students have acquired a desired attitude if they consistently choose to engage in behaviors that express the desired attitude. For example, if the goal is to convince students to be self-regulated learners, students who, without being asked to do so, set mastery goals, reflect on their learning process, seek opportunities for practice and feedback, and adapt their learning approaches based on the task, the time available, and their past results, have acquired the desired attitude.

More specifically, attitude experts conceptualize changes in student attitudes along a wide spectrum as depicted in Illustration 5-1.

At one end of the spectrum, the student merely engages in behavior that evidences the attitude. At the opposite end of the spec-

Illustration 5-1. Spectrum of Behavior Evidencing Attitude Change

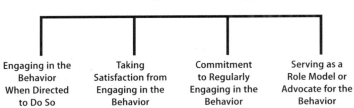

| Engaging in the Behavior When Directed to Do So | Taking Satisfaction from Engaging in the Behavior | Commitment to Regularly Engaging in the Behavior | Serving as a Role Model or Advocate for the Behavior |

trum, the student has become so committed to the attitude that the student has become a role model or advocate for the behavior. In the middle of this spectrum are lesser degrees of dedication to the value, such as taking satisfaction when engaging in the behavior or committing to the behavior (choosing to engage in the behavior when no one else is watching).

It's also helpful to conceptualize attitude change in terms of three fundamental principles or elements: cognition, affect, and behavior. Cognition refers to knowing how to implement the new attitude. Affect refers to knowing why the behavior is valuable and therefore worthy of adoption. Behavior is implementing the attitude, especially if the person chooses to do so in the face of competing demands.

Techniques for Producing Attitude Change

Three commonly-used techniques have been shown to influence attitudes: persuasion (trying to convince students to change by arguments and other messages), role modeling (using others to demonstrate the efficacy of adopting the attitude), and experience (creating an occurrence that juxtaposes the benefits of the desired attitude with students' existing attitudes). The discussion below considers each of these possibilities in the order of least to most effective. Persuasion is the least effective technique and, in fact, can be ineffective if the students are highly committed to their existing views. Experience is the most effective technique, especially if the experience positively juxtaposes the desired attitude against the students' previously held attitudes. Role modeling is somewhere in the middle in terms of its effectiveness.

Persuasion

Persuasion has two facets: the characteristics of the arguments and the source of the arguments. Each of these facets is addressed below.

Effective arguments for change must be easy to understand, well-structured, and convincing, but the key to success is whether the arguments address a problem the students regard as personally significant. Because the students often do not perceive that they have a problem based on their existing beliefs and attitudes, it is helpful to think of persuasion as needing to address two issues: (1) the existence of a problem, and (2) the advocated behavior that addresses the problem. Finally, the research suggests that persuasion is most effective if the persuader explicitly articulates the attitude change for which he is arguing.

The source of the argument refers to the person who is making the argument (the speaker or the author of the argument). A source is most effective when it has one or both of two characteristics: credibility (expertise or education) and attractiveness (similarity to students or fame). The research recommends that teachers expressly establish the persuader's credibility. Accordingly, if you use a guest practitioner as a persuader, for example, make sure you tell the students about the speaker's expertise.

Upper-division students are commonly used for persuasion because of their similarity to new students. How many times have you had students adopt even crazy suggestions from an upper-division law student (usually someone they bumped into in the student lunchroom) who claims to have done well in your class or to know "the secret" for doing well in your class? Using upper-division students allows you to undo some of the damage done by these lunchroom experts.

If you choose to use attractive persuaders, select a diverse group of persuaders and encourage them to open up with the students. A major factor in attractiveness is whether the students perceive that the persuader shares their attitudes with respect to issues other than those about which the persuader is speaking. By selecting a diverse group of persuaders and encouraging the persuaders to be open about themselves, their career goals, and their values, you increase the number of students who are likely to be influenced.

While persuasion can be effective and probably is the most commonly-used attitude-change technique, it typically only addresses the affective elements of attitude change, i.e., persuaders only address why an attitude change is a good idea. Modeling adds in the cognitive element.

Modeling

In the context of law school, modeling refers to having a former student or a practitioner demonstrate the desired attitude and being rewarded for doing so. Credibility is as important for modeling as it is for persuasion. High credibility role models, people the students regard as worthy of imitation, are particularly effective. Effective role modeling enables students to observe the role model engaging in the behavior *and* observe the role model being reinforced for doing so. The combination of demonstration and observed reinforcement emphasizes the relationship between the two. For example, if students see a successful upper-division student engaging in self-regulated learning and witness the student being rewarded by good grades or exciting career opportunities, they are more likely to adopt the desired behavior. In this way, modeling addresses both the cognitive and the affective elements of attitude change.

Law professors have three potential sources of role models. First, you function as a role model, representing the profession to your students. For example, your professionalism and commitment in fulfilling your teaching role communicates your values. Students quickly decide whether you are engaged, prepared, and committed. In addition, students notice whether you practice what you preach in terms of service to our communities, institutions, peers, and them.

Second, upper-division students are very convincing to other students. Accordingly, having upper-division students demonstrate, for example, their efforts at reflecting on the learning process, and then publically expressing your admiration for their

efforts, can be effective in convincing students to become more reflective about their own learning processes. It would be hard, of
course, for your upper-division students to model (during a class
session) behaviors reflecting values such as professionalism and
public service. The students may, instead, need to describe what
they do outside of class and how they have been rewarded, such as
by developing networking connections.

Third, other practitioners make excellent role models. In particular, we suggest using former students who have become successful practitioners. For example, having an alumnus reflect on
something he did in practice (take a deposition, argue a motion,
try a case) and brainstorm how he will change his approach the
next time he needs to perform a similar task may be an effective
act of role modeling. Similarly, having a practitioner discuss her
plans to do pro bono work and then report back on her experience
can be effective. In this way, the practitioner helps students transfer the adoption of the value in law school to the form the value
takes in law practice.

Role models are even more effective if the students try out the
behavior themselves. Students who try out the new behaviors reflecting the desired value are likely to adopt that value because the
activity both engages them and addresses the behavioral element
of attitude change and development. Experience addresses all three
elements of behavioral change.

Experience

Experience refers to students trying out the desired behavior
and experiencing its benefits for themselves. Experiences are most
effective if the conflict between the students' existing values and
the desired value is readily identifiable and the students receive or
discover the benefits from engaging in the alternative behavior. Because such experiences expose a discrepancy between the students'
existing values and the desired value, many educational researchers
use the term "dissonance" to refer to this strategy.

The challenge is to design experiences that are authentic, give
students as much autonomy in the process as possible, and allow

students to experience the benefits of adopting the desired value. An experience is authentic if the students are engaging in the behavior in a way that is as similar to how they might act in the future. For example, using actual course feedback (e.g., a grade on a paper, comments on a practice exam) as a springboard for getting students to engage in self-regulation increases the likelihood students will make the connection between the self-regulation activity and their other efforts at learning. An experience gives students autonomy if the students have some choice in the process. For example, asking students to engage in public service but to choose for themselves the particular form of public service gives students autonomy and increases the likelihood that they will value the experience they have chosen. If the students do not experience any reward from adopting the behavior, experience is unlikely to change their attitudes. On the other hand, if, for example, the students get a sense they are learning more by reflecting on their learning processes, they are more likely to adopt this behavior as their own. Such natural rewards, rewards inherent in adopting the desired attitude, are more effective than grades or other extrinsic rewards because the natural rewards develop student's intrinsic interest in adopting the behavior.

Experience can address all three elements of behavioral change. Experience addresses the behavioral element of attitude change because the students are actually implementing the desired behavior. Experience also addresses the cognitive element because the students are trying out the techniques for themselves and can receive coaching in their efforts at implementation. Experience may most effectively address the affective element of change because, rather than being told about the benefits or seeing someone else get the benefits from implementing the desired behavior, the students actually experience the benefits for themselves.

Checklist for Teaching for Motivation and Attitude Change

Illustration 5-2 is a checklist for teaching for motivation and attitude change. This checklist summarizes things law professors can do to better motivated students.

Illustration 5-2. Teaching for Motivation and Attitude Change Checklist

❏   Adopt attitudinal strategies
    ❏   Passion and enthusiasm
    ❏   Confidence

❏   Create authentic lawyering experiences

❏   Use variety of teaching techniques

❏   Structure opportunities for student autonomy

❏   Encourage student goal-setting

❏   Create non-threatening challenge, incongruity, and conflict to spark interest

❏   Provide reinforcement

❏   Find optimal role models

❏   Make sure students try out both the desired behavior and receive rewards for engaging in it

You will find examples of the concepts from this chapter in Appendix 5 on the book's website—http://lawteaching.org/resources.

Appendix 5-1: Role Plays

Appendix 5-2: Experiential Professionalism Instruction

Appendix 5-3: Time Management/Self-Monitoring Log

Appendix 5-4: Post-Assessment Reflection Exercises

Chapter 6

Teaching the Class

This chapter focuses on the nuts and bolts of "live" teaching—when you and the students are all physically present in one location. Bear in mind that there is no single way to teach the class effectively; the goal is to have effective classes for most students most of the time.

Keep one fundamental question in mind as you teach your class:

"Who in the room is acting like a lawyer?"

Keeping this question paramount in your mind as you teach will help you focus on your learning goals and maximize students' experience. The more the students are *engaged in acting like lawyers—speaking and doing—the more they are likely to learn.*

A related question about live teaching is,

"Who is doing most of the talking in class?"

Conventional teaching focuses on *what the teachers do* in the classroom—what the teacher says and how the teacher presents information or questions. To enhance student learning, focus on a different *image: **Teaching is creating a place in which students learn.*** Creating a place in which students learn means that your role in the classroom is **less** about what you say and **more about what students are doing.** In the classroom, try to ensure that most students are acting like lawyers as they engage in applying the learning objectives you have identified. This chapter suggests ways to make this happen.

Create a Positive Learning Environment Where Students Feel Safe Taking Risks

Before considering the "nuts and bolts" of teaching, consider the "art" side of live teaching, the "feel" of the class. Creating a positive learning environment is critical to student learning and takes more than teaching technique and subject matter expertise. Below are some suggestions about what you can do to help build a positive classroom environment.

Know and Use Students' Names

If you have a hard time learning names, practice with flash cards. If learning students' names quickly is not feasible, we recommend that you use name cards (see Illustration 6-1) so that you can regularly use students' names during the class.

Practice students' names outside of class—a few minutes a day. Regular practice, a commitment to learning students' names, and using name cards enables most teachers to learn students' names within a few weeks, even in classes of over 100 students.

Be Conscious of the Messages You Send

Communication experts tell us that we convey significant messages through our body language and tone of voice. When in the classroom, be aware of what your body language may convey to students. Eye contact, listening attentively, and projecting a sense of confidence and openness are as important as any specific technique.

Find a way to see students positively. You may think of them as friends you have invited to a dinner party, offspring, or young relatives (how would I respond if my favorite niece asked that question?). Consider them future colleagues in practice or on the bench. Whatever you do, find something to be positive about.

Illustration 6-1. Name Cards

Using Name Cards

In classes of more than twenty, we find it helpful to have students bring "table tents" or "UN Name Cards" to class. These name cards have students' names printed in large font on the front and back. With the names on both sides, students can learn each others' names.

These cards are printed on heavy card stock paper so that they stand up and last for at least a few weeks. A faculty administrative assistant can print these off your rosters. On the first day of class, you distribute the name cards and make a heavy black marker available to those who want to be called by a different name.

Alternatively you can bring in photocopy paper, ask students to fold in half lengthwise and write their names in ALL CAPS on both sides, using a heavy black marker.

Encourage students to bring the name cards to class until you know all their names — even better, wait until all students know each others' names. (Sophie asks students to put the name cards in a book they regularly bring to class or tape to the back of their laptop so that they always have them readily available.) The table tents help you and the students attach names to faces starting on the first day of class.

Be Enthusiastic

Students greatly appreciate it when you project confidence and enthusiasm, and you can always find something to be enthusiastic about. Show enthusiasm with small gestures: start the class with a smile and "Good evening!" Students enjoy learning from teachers who clearly like students and teaching.

Model Taking Risks and Acknowledging Weaknesses

Students respect and appreciate teachers who are self-confident and acknowledge their weaknesses. It's ok to say, "Great question.

I never thought of that. I'll have to think about it and get back to you." If you are trying something new, tell students something like, "I'm going out on a limb here. I am not sure if this exercise will work, but I am going to ask you to engage in a different kind of learning exercise today."

When you make a mistake (we've all made tons), acknowledge it. "Last class I gave you some misinformation. Let me try to clarify." Let them know that you, too, have to work at writing complex prose, speaking in public, and teaching effectively. Apologize when you err. Admitting your errors and asking for students' pardon treats students with respect.

Be Transparent and Authentic

Explain to students what you are doing and why. Even if students want a concrete answer to an unresolved issue, explain why the answer is "it depends" and what it depends on. When you use different instructional activities, explain why, at least the first few times you use them. Be honest and direct. You may say that there is no right answer, but you mean there is no *one* single right answer. Instead there is a cluster of right answers and a group of wrong ones.

As the educator Parker Palmer says, "We teach who we are." If your style is to be self-deprecating and you are good at telling jokes, do so. Don't try to be someone you are not. It often takes several years of teaching to develop your teaching persona. Pay attention and be patient.

The Nuts and Bolts

This part of the chapter has four main sections:

- Pre-class—the fifteen minutes before class starts
- Openings—the first five minutes
- Body—the heart of the class session (instructional activities)
  - Active learning exercises
  - Lectures
  - Questioning techniques

- Visuals
- Discovery sequence instruction
- Timing
- Closings—the last five minutes

In class, tell students what you want them to learn (opening of class), engage them in instructional exercises to help them learn (body), and summarize what you wanted them to learn (closing).

Pre-Class: The 15 Minutes before Class Starts— Arrive Early

Showing up 10–15 minutes before class allows you to take care of any problems and shows that you are interested in the students. For the first class, figure out how you plan to use the room. Practice using the technology, including chalk or markers. Make sure everyone will have a seat and can see the board or screen. If all systems are working, use the time to set out materials, project first slides, or write your objectives on the board. In the remaining time, chat with the early students, take a deep breath, or focus on your learning goals.

Openings: The First Five Minutes of Class—Provide an Overview

The beginning of class sets the tone and prepares your students to learn. Make a positive first impression—show students your enthusiasm, confidence and respect. Some specific suggestions:

Provide Students with the Objectives at the Beginning of Class

Give students the "road map" of the class. Using two ways of providing information, such as visually and verbally, makes it more likely students will retain it. Visually show the class learning goals on a slide, a handout, or on the board. Verbally flesh out the objectives and provide the context of the class in the learning unit and the course. For example you could say:

> In the last few classes we analyzed a range of crimes, ending with murder. We looked at what a prosecutor would need to prove to charge a defendant with negligent homicide, manslaughter, felony murder, and first- and second-degree murder. In groups you made arguments applying the elements of those felonies to different factual situations.
>
> Today we are moving to conspiracy. Specifically, today we are investigating prosecution and defendant arguments for conspiracy and attempted conspiracy. We will be building upon the same skills—articulating the law, facts and policy—in making and responding to arguments.

You can further explain what will be happening in the body of the class:

> Today you will be working with one partner to compare and analyze your individual responses to Problem 7-A, using cases A, B, and C.

See If Students Have Any Questions Arising from the Previous Class Sessions

After you've asked if students have any questions, pause and mentally count to five to allow students a chance to gather their thoughts. If you don't want to respond to any questions, don't ask. If students have many questions, answer a few of them and then move on, encouraging students to email you, talk to you after class, or post questions or comments on a course webpage.

Administrative Matters

Find out what your institution requires for tracking attendance, and take attendance at the beginning of class. One of the easiest ways to do this is to circulate a list of the enrolled students next to which students can sign their names.

Modifications—First Day of the Course; Other Significant Classes

The First Day of the Course

The first day of the course is special. Your opening may be longer, giving you time to tell a story about the course, practice, or yourself.

Explain any policies for attendance, seating, and using names. Some teachers like to be called "Professor X," others are comfortable with a range of names. You can say:

My name is Pat Davis. You can call me Pat, Ms. Davis or Professor Davis. I will call you by whatever name you prefer. Today I will go through the roster; let me know if I have mispronounced your name or if you have a different name you would like to use.

Explain your views on teaching and ask for students' help:

We'll be using a variety of teaching and learning strategies in this class. I will lecture, ask you to do group work, in-class exercises, and practice other lawyering skills. You all have different learning preferences and not all techniques may be ideal for you. I ask for your forbearance when we are using a style that works for others, but not for you.

When Students Face Crises or Distractions

Delay the formal opening to allow a time for reflection, silence, and a chance to discuss. Whether a student has become severely ill or lost a family member, or a catastrophe has hit the area, acknowledge the crisis and give students some quiet time.

As most of you may have heard, last night terrible storms attacked the west coast. I know that many of you have been concerned about family and friends who were in the area and whom you have had a hard time contacting. Let's take

five minutes to sit in silence or write. At the end of that time,
anyone who wants to can share thoughts about this tragedy.

If this isn't your style, you might just want to acknowledge the event and move on. Be authentic and remember that students crave to connect with our humanity.

I heard about the shooting in City X yesterday and am very
sorry for all those involved. If any of you would like to talk
to me about it outside of class, I would be happy to do so.

Similarly, acknowledge challenges facing students. Many students become stressed and tired in November and March as they face final exam pressure. Acknowledge that stress and invite them to focus on the class.

OK, so many of you are preoccupied. For now, I am going to
ask you to set those concerns aside for the next 40 minutes
and practice being securities lawyers.

Body — The Heart of the Class Session

The body of a class session is where you will be spending the most time, focusing on what you want students to learn by the end of the class. The body of the class is the total class time minus about ten minutes (five minutes for the opening and five for the closing.) Keep your class outline and learning objectives present on a handout, slide or board; this will make you less likely to try to cover too much material or go off on too many tangents.

Focus on One to Three Learning Objectives per One-Hour Class Session

Once you have identified the learning objectives for each class (Chapter 4), work backwards to design effective class sessions. For example, if you want students to outline the steps involved in registering a new trademark, identify what they need to do and how you will know whether they have correctly outlined the steps. Sketch out how much time you want to have students work on each class objective. Remember that they are more likely to retain a deep understanding of this process if they are actively engaged.

Active Learning Exercises

Use active learning exercises that engage students, helping them practice acting like lawyers.

Students are engaged when they are:

- Writing
- Talking and listening
- Reading
- Reflecting
- Demonstrating

Illustration 6-2 lists five active learning instructional activities you can use in the body of your class. Each of these activities is described briefly below. When they are engaged in these activities, the students, and not just the teacher, are "doing the work"—practicing acting like lawyers. They are actively solving problems, thinking, talking, listening, taking notes, reading, and writing. When you use these techniques, watch the energy, volume, and activity in the class soar. More information about ways to use experiential learning techniques— real-world experiences and simulations is included in Chapter 7.

**Illustration 6-2. Instructional Activities:
Active Learning Selections**

- **Think-write-pair-share**
- **Small group discussion**
- **Student-to-student group discussion**
- **Small group role-playing**
- **Point/counterpoint**

You don't need to be an expert in these activities to be an effective teacher. Many simple, quick techniques can be included in law school classes. Start simple, start small, and give yourself time to work these into your classes and learn from experiences. For each class, remember to ask yourself, "Who in this room is acting like a lawyer?" *and* "Who in this room is talking?" *Choose one or two new active learning exercises a semester. Don't give up just because they didn't work as well as you hoped the first time or some students didn't like them.*

Ideally, use three or more different instructional activities per class. Variety keeps the class interesting, engages students in different levels of thinking, and addresses different learning preferences. Consider Socratic-style questioning as one kind of instructional activity (more on Socratic-style questioning below) and mix it with other instructional activities.

Think-Write-Pair-Share

This technique is one of the quickest, easiest, and most versatile active learning exercises. Pose a question verbally or in writing. Ask students to think about the question for a minute and then jot down a response. Once they have completed their responses (one-to-three minutes depending on the question's complexity) ask students to exchange their ideas with a neighbor. Ask them to discuss their answers and the reasons for them (one–three minutes).

Call on a few students to provide responses, or ask one or two students to volunteer his or her neighbor's response. Note responses on the board, enter and project them on a screen, or verbally reinforce responses. After students have talked with a neighbor, who has either acknowledged confusion with the issue or affirmed the student's response, a much greater range of students volunteer and are comfortable being called on.

Small-Group Discussion

Pose a question or problem that students must work together to solve. Students can collectively discuss and answer questions at different levels of thinking, e.g., What are the elements of the statute? Which element is at issue in this client's case? How would you describe federal preemption to a lay person?

As the groups work, you may decide to circulate among them, be available as a resource for students to call upon, sit in and listen to a few groups, or allow them to work on their own. If you circulate, you can identify and address any common areas of confusion and get a sense of how the groups are functioning. If you allow the groups to work on their own, at least some of your students may be more likely to take risks. Once groups have discussed their responses, call on a couple of different students—ideally those who have previously not contributed to the large group discussion—to talk about the group's responses. Once you have a response, invite students who had a different response to contribute.

A word about using small groups effectively. Small group assignments must have crystal clear directions. Specify an amount of time for students to work in groups. Allow less time than you think students will need, and add time if students are still focused and more time would help them attain the learning goals. You can gauge how things are going by asking the class as a whole or circulating and asking different groups whether they would like another couple of minutes. If all the groups are working on the same problem, avoid having groups do a "reporting back" where each group gives a presentation on the same topic. (The reporting back group responses get tiresome and most students disengage after a few minutes.)

Student-to-Student Group Discussion

Ask the students to lead the discussion by calling on each other. For example, after posing a question about a rule, factual analysis or other teaching objective, explain to students that the goal of the next few minutes is for them to achieve that objective by talking to and calling on each other without your involvement. You can start the discussion by asking a student, perhaps one who has previously not spoken, to respond to the question you have posed. After she or he has contributed, each subsequent student must call on the next one to further the discussion. While students talk and refine their understanding, you or another student can serve as scribe and note responses on the board.

Small Group Role-Playing and Simulations

Divide the class in sections, and assign a role to each. For example, in an employment law class, you might assign one group to the role of employees, one to employers, one to in-house counsel, and one to legislators. In small groups, ask the students to collectively outline the large-scale structure of their positions, using notes or bullet points. Tell them to think about the big picture, not get stuck on the particular words or polished language and note that they may want to start in the middle or end and bounce around as they work through the outline. One or two groups from each section could write their outline on chart paper, overheads, board, or laptop, and then show the analysis to the whole class.

Point/Counterpoint

Divide the class in half, with half the students representing one party and half another, and ask students to take turns making their arguments. In this portion of the session, ask a participant on one side of the room to make one statement in support of an argument, and then identify someone on the opposite side of the room who will make a statement either refuting the argument or making a different argument supporting the opposite outcome. Continue for a few minutes as both sides of the room explore the analysis. At the end of this portion, ask students to raise their hands to identify, given the materials they have, what the strongest arguments are. You can also do this exercise with a small prop, such as a squishy ball or soft toy that students toss back and forth across the room. Emphasize that the idea is to toss gently to another student, rather than demonstrate throwing prowess.

Additional Points about Instructional Activities

Keep Track of the Time

Active learning instructional activities can take on a life of their own. Help keep students on task and focused on the learning objectives. If individual or groups of students finish an activity early, have additional instructional activities they can engage in.

Close the Loop

After students have engaged in learning activities, explain what they have done and reinforce the learning you have observed. You can summarize main points, invite students to share what they learned, or clarify students' questions.

Sometimes it is hard to reconvene the class as a whole once students have engaged in active learning. Techniques to reconvene class include briefly turning on and off the lights, calling students' attention to the class, giving students a warning about how many minutes they have left, and using their names "I see that Carlos's and Kim's groups are ready to discuss their responses with the class.... Others?"

Lectures

Lectures can lead to significant student learning. They are most effective when they are:

- Short (10–15 minutes max)
- Add valuable content
- Surrounded by other activities
- Supported by visuals
- Delivered effectively

Use Micro-Lectures—10 to 15 Minutes

Studies show that, within ten minutes, students' attention considerably drops off. No matter how dynamic we are as speakers, few people retain more than a small portion of a lecture. Mini-lectures are highly effective in addressing students' misconceptions about a concept, giving feedback to students, or summarizing a portion of the class. Mini-lectures are most effective when you give them *after* students have done some preparation and engaged in problem solving. Then students are primed to pay attention; they realize where they need guidance.

Add Valuable Content

Don't include in a lecture anything you can put in print unless doing so will likely help students learn. Instead, build upon what you have assigned students to prepare, or highlight important points that were not in written material or may need emphasis.

Surround Micro-Lectures with Other Activities

Sandwich micro-lectures between a small group discussion, active learning technique, or other activities that engage your students. Include pauses between main points to allow students to catch up on notes, review, and consolidate their thinking.

Include Visuals

Use pictures, graphics, props and other material—widely available on the internet—to reinforce important points. Consider giving students a barebones outline or chart into which they can take notes; the mental effort students use to complete the outline helps hold their attention.

Deliver Micro-Lectures Effectively

Use a voice audible from the back of the room. Vary your phrasing and allow for pauses. Avoid speaking in a monotone. Move around. Make eye contact with students. Periodically include students' names, "So if Marcella was filing a patent claim, she would …" Tell students which points are especially important and encourage them to write them down. Repeat main points during the micro-lecture to reorient novice learners.

Questioning Techniques

Using questions or engaging in "Socratic" dialogue can be one of the most effective ways to engage students in achieving all levels of critical thinking. One of the greatest weaknesses of traditional law school Socratic-style discussion is that most students are not engaged. Certainly, the selected student is actively engaged in the one-on-one conversation with the teacher and receives feedback on her learning process. For all the other students in the class the learning process is vicarious at best. Some students are shopping electronically, e-mailing other professors, or sending each other messages unrelated to class. Ways to make Socratic-style questioning effective and engaging:

- Prepare students in advance
- Ask clear questions, one at a time
- Ask a range of questions
- Allow sufficient wait-time (three seconds or more)
- Encourage effective responses and respond appropriately to ineffective answers

Prepare Students in Advance

From handouts, web pages, syllabi, or other formats, give students enough information in advance so that they are prepared to discuss the questions. (See Chapters 3, 4, and 5.) For more complex thinking skills, giving students core questions in advance will help them target their out-of-class studying.

Model the kinds of responses you want. For example, present students with a problem and then model how you would solve the problem, talking through each step, and admitting where you are stumped in the process. Pause as you go, allowing students to catch up with you and take notes.

Ask Clear Questions

Write down the questions in advance to ensure they align with your class learning objectives. For students who struggle to learn from oral presentations, or speak English as a second language, projecting your questions on a PowerPoint slide or writing on the board will allow the students to more readily process the question. If you have a definite point you want a student to make, state a proposition and ask students whether and why they agree or disagree.

Help students by naming what you want them learn, such as by asking, "The court used a number of factors in rejecting the claim for punitive damages. I'm wondering if you all identified the same factors, or interpreted this opinion differently. Phil, please start us off by identifying one of the factors that the court seems to use." If you don't wish to call on a particular student, invite any student to respond, "Could someone start …?"

Ask One Question at a Time

If you see students' blank looks after asking a question, resist throwing out other questions, or tacking on additional points. Discipline yourself to staying with one question at a time. Repeat a question if it is long or complex, but don't add questions as it will compound student confusion. Writing questions out in advance helps avoiding such problems.

Ask a Range of Questions

Open-ended questions are more likely to generate discussion than yes/no questions. Vary the kind of question and the length of time it takes students to respond. As you progress through the course, ask students questions at increasingly more complex levels.

Embed material about a concept studied earlier in a question about the current class topic, for example: "Let's review the tests administrative agencies use to … [name tests briefly]. Let's apply those factors to …"

Allow Sufficient Wait-Time (at Least Three to Five Seconds) after You Ask a Question

Most of us struggle with silence in the classroom. The research shows that we usually wait only a second or two before we fill the silence by making a comment or rephrasing the question. One second is not enough time for most students to generate a meaningful response. Giving yourself and students time to process the question usually results in more students being able to answer your question. You can explain this fact to students to address the awkwardness of the quiet. "I am going to wait for 5 seconds to give you time to think," or, "I see that Ee Ming and Rafael have answers to this question. How about some others? I'll wait."

Another way to provide students with time to process the question is to ask them to write a response in 30 seconds or to engage in a think-write-pair-share exercise as described above. These processes allow students a chance to reflect and work through their thinking for a particular response.

Encourage and Promote Effective Responses, Respond Appropriately to Ineffective Answers

When a student responds to a question, stop moving and look at the student, leaning slightly toward him or her. Acknowledge students' effective responses, both when they respond and later, e.g., "Remember Louisa's excellent point about …" Invite students to develop their responses. "Great start! Now can you help me out by explaining how you arrived at that answer?" Smile, nod, be quiet, and make eye contact to help students elaborate their response. Write students' responses on the board, and invite others to help their classmates to build student confidence in responding to questions. Acknowledge students' insights that are new to you; your students will appreciate your respect for them and your self-confidence in your expertise.

When students give a "wrong" answer, guide them to a better response, if at all possible. Focus on the answer, not on the student, and acknowledge any positive aspect of the response. Using a gentle sense of humor can also help diffuse a potentially uncomfortable moment for the student, "Oh, good, that is so-o-o close! But I am wondering if that answer might be missing something. How about taking a look further down the page where it says …." Try hints (e.g., "Why do you think the court mentioned _____ fact?") or cues (e.g., "Is there anything in the federal rules that you might use as a basis for support in making your argument?"). You can also invite the student to ask for "co-counsel" to assist, and then return to the student to have the student end the discussion with a positive contribution.

Visuals

In this section we address a couple of visual attributes of the classroom, including PowerPoint and dress.

PowerPoint and Other Visuals

To include visuals that will help students learn, keep in mind a few essentials. For any visual device, whether a computer projection, movie clip, or black or white board, the key is whether all students can "read" the visual. Check out the sight lines from all points in the room. Less is more. Use bigger letters, numbers, and images. Have fewer of them.

When projecting text, apply principles of effective graphics:

- Use text boxes, bullets, white space, numbered lists, and color.
- Use a font without feet like **Arial** or Calibri—these are easier to read when enlarged.

- Limit text to six lines of type or less, which increases the like-lihood your students can read your text.
- Limit the text to the important points. Include additional points on another slide, or amplify the material verbally.
- Unless there is a good reason for doing so, when you are in the classroom, don't look at the projected text and read it. Instead, face the students, use the text as a focal point, and then engage students in discussion.

If you are using any kind of a projected image, practice the technology in advance and be prepared to have an alternate plan when the technology fails.

A final thought about using PowerPoint. It is tempting to use PowerPoint slides solely to transmit information—e.g., the language of a statute or the three points you want to make in a lecture. If you only transmit knowledge using PowerPoint, however, your students may conclude that your course is mostly or exclusively about acquiring knowledge. By including questions, problems, visual metaphors, or even a checklist that addresses the process of using a skill you are teaching, you communicate a much different message about what's important in your class.

Dress

Dress is an issue for all teachers. For teachers who don't fit the traditional profile of a law professor, dress is especially important. Some suggestions:

There Is No One Right Way to Dress

What you choose to wear to the classroom will depend on your personality, your institution, your comfort level, and your students.

Consider the Dress Culture at Your Institution

If you have questions, talk to your colleagues about these unspoken norms. If you want ideas about how your students might perceive teachers your age, look at media images of people in authority.

Wear Comfortable Clothing That Makes You Feel Confident

Putting on a suit can create confidence: "Even if I am scared out of my wits, I'll at least look the part of a law professor." Some women feel most confident wearing pants; others feel they project a desired image of professionalism when they wear skirts. Similarly, some men feel better wearing a jacket; others feel confident so long as they wear a collared shirt and tie *or* jacket but don't feel a need for both. Whatever you decide to wear, try it out before you wear it in the classroom.

Adjust Your Clothing during the Semester, if Appropriate

Most of us are more formal at the beginning of the semester, when we want to make the best first impression with our students. As the semester continues, and students start to show stress, you may want to adopt more casual attire. One teacher pulls out his cardigan sweaters for those days.

Discovery Sequence Instruction

Discovery sequence instruction involves providing students a series of examples and non-examples of a concept and labeling each as either an example or non-example and then asking students to infer the principle or principles that reconcile the examples and non-examples. For example, provide students a set of examples and non-examples of contracts to which Article II of the UCC would apply or of activities for which a person successfully could be charged with conspiracy and then ask students to infer the principles. You could also provide students with a set of effective and ineffective responses to a hypothetical and ask the students to explain the principles that distinguish the effective responses.

Timing

Map out and prioritize chunks of time along with your learning objectives. For example, you might divide a 50-minute class into three sections of 13 minutes each, leaving 10 minutes for the opening and closing of the class session. Rather than setting the exact timing for each instructional activity, consider what you want students to have been doing for each 13-minute chunk of time. **Remember, you want students to be the ones acting like lawyers in the class.**

Many of us worry that we have enough material to "fill the time." If you are focusing on **what the students are doing,** you will wonder instead how you can help students learn sophisticated skills within the body of class.

For example, you have 40 minutes for the body of class. You plan the following:

- Small group discussion: 7 minutes
- Whole class discussion: 6 minutes
- Mini-lecture summarizing and clarifying: 10 minutes
- Think-Write-Pair-Share: 3 minutes
- Whole class discussion: 14 minutes

In the classroom, however, you find that students need more time in the small group discussions. Because students seem engaged and on task, you extend the time to ten minutes. If you get behind, go back to your learning objectives. What is it that students should learn by the end of this class? Of the instructional activities you have planned, which one is most likely to help students achieve those learning objectives in the time left? Rather than cramming all the instructional activities into the remaining time, scrap one or more of those activities and focus on the one that you think will be most effective. If you plan for this in advance, you can determine which instructional activities you definitely want students to engage in, and which ones are not essential, but would be lovely to use if time allows.

Respect the majority of the students by focusing the discussion on what students should be learning in class. One technique to help keep students on task and limit discussion is saying something like, "Last comment goes to Jo," even when three other people have their hands in the air. Another is stating, "Let's hear two more contributions. I'd like to hear from students who have not yet contributed to the class discussion." If you have decided not to call on volunteers who are the most frequent contributors, talk to them outside of class, letting them know that you appreciate their eagerness and enthusiasm, and that you want to be sure a variety of students' voices are heard in class.

If you have extra time in class, return to your learning objectives. Because being able to articulate ideas in writing is such an important lawyering skill, even if students are "done" with the discussion, ask students to prepare an outline summarizing key points. When students have to move beyond talking to writing and organizing, they frequently identify gaps in their analysis. Another solution is to prepare an "extra" instructional activity that you use during the class if you have time.

It is hard to know how the class will go. Spend time before class rehearsing, refining and tracking how long it takes. No matter what else you do, **end the class on time**. Track time so that you leave five minutes at the end for the closing.

Closings: The Last Five Minutes of Class

Use the last five minutes of class to consolidate students' learning, mirroring the opening. Three examples are below.

Summarize Key Points

In the last few minutes of class, summarize the key learning points by using a skeletal outline on the board or a slide and verbally adding to it. (This may be the same outline or slide that you used at the beginning of class.)

Today you focused on the skill of identifying ambiguity in contracts. You noticed ambiguities in the words used, such as "damage to property or physical injury." The phrase was ambiguous because "damage" alone included physical and economic damage. You also noticed ambiguities created by ... [continues]

You noticed ambiguities I hadn't seen and other classes hadn't seen. You learned that, while this effort may seem picky in a class, it can cost a party millions of dollars. You've discussed what steps you could take as lawyers to identify ambiguity in drafting contracts.

You've worked through all but the final, most complex problem. Please review that for next class; we'll start with that problem and then move on to the next topic....
Thank you and see you Monday.

Give Students Time to Consolidate Their Learning

Involve the students in reflecting and consolidating the class objectives.

Today you evaluated different proposed temporary restraining orders. In your groups, you saw five examples of how these might be drafted, and evaluated the effectiveness of different versions. Now I'd like you to take a minute to write a few notes to yourself. If in practice or on an exam you needed to draft a proposed temporary restraining order, what important things would you want to remind yourself to do?

Allow students a few minutes to write. Then ask students to compare their notes with someone else, or invite the class as a whole to contribute a few important points.

Allow Students to Reflect on Their Learning

This closing lets students practice the skills they need to become independent learners.

Today, you were assigned to play the roles of constituents seeking to resolve a toxic landfill problem. Some of you rep-

resented the landowner, others the neighbors, the city, legis-
lators, the company that produced the toxins, and consumers
who would benefit from the toxins. Think about and then
write down one thing you learned from this exercise.

As with the previous suggestion, you could then invite students to compare their notes with each other, share with the whole class, or thank the students for participating and let them leave when they have finished writing.

Closing Modification: The Very Last Class— Leave Ten to Fifteen Minutes for the Final Closing

The last class, like the first class, is special. Some teachers like to summarize the course, talking about what the students have learned, thanking students for their efforts, and revealing what the teacher most appreciated about sharing the learning with this group of students. Other teachers use the last class as a chance to build students' confidence. They may tell students about the mistakes they made in their lives, and give ideas about how to navigate the stress of final exams. They may tell stories about practice and life. They may offer their assistance and support for future years. They may ask a final question. One of our colleagues stands at the door and shakes the hand of each exiting student. Like any other aspect of teaching, be authentic. Do something you enjoy doing, and try different approaches to ending the course.

Final Notes on Teaching the Class

All teachers have good days and bad days. Don't seek "perfection." You are the single most expensive, most adaptive, most empathic educational resource available to your students to learn what they need to learn in your course. Consider the small steps you can take to help students act as lawyers in the classroom. Reflect and learn from the experience.

Checklist for Teaching the Class

Illustration 6-3 is a checklist you can use for teaching the class.

Illustration 6-3. Teaching the Class Checklist

❑ **Consider:**
❑ **Who in the room is acting like a lawyer?**
❑ **Who is doing most of the talking in the class?**

    ❑ **Create a positive learning environment**
        ❑ Know and use students' names
        ❑ Be conscious of the messages you send
        ❑ Be enthusiastic
        ❑ Model taking risks and acknowledging weaknesses
        ❑ Envision yourself as a "guide on the side"
        ❑ Be transparent
        ❑ Be authentic

    ❑ **Openings—the first five minutes**
        ❑ Arrive early
        ❑ Consider the opening message you send
        ❑ Modify for first and other special days

    ❑ **Body—the heart of the class session**
        ❑ Use a variety of instructional activities
        ❑ Use activities that engage the students
        ❑ Use mini-lectures surrounded by other activities
        ❑ Use effective questioning techniques
        ❑ Address controversial issues
        ❑ Use visuals students can "read"
        ❑ Prioritize your timing according to learning objectives

    ❑ **Closings—the last five minutes**
        ❑ Summarize and consolidate students' learning
        ❑ Modify for the last class

    ❑ **Engage in ongoing practice, reflection and evaluation**

You will find examples of the concepts from this chapter in Appendix 6 on the book's website—http://lawteaching.org/resources.

Appendix 6-1: Discovery Sequence Exercises
    Duty to Disclose Discovery Sequence Exercise
    Binding vs. Persuasive Authority Discovery Sequence
       Exercise

Chapter 7

Experiential Teaching and Learning

Introduction

Through real-life exercises, students engage in the complexity of practice, gain a deeper understanding of the context of legal problems, practice a variety of skills and values, start to recognize areas of confusion, and become actively involved in their learning. For example, a photo of a nuclear waste facility located next a river may have a powerful effect on students' understanding of environmental law. Simulations are particularly effective for some students; students who struggle with learning through verbal discussion and reading and writing often excel when they are asked to simulate the role of an attorney. Experiential exercises can also help students gain the kind of authentic confidence that comes from competence. And because real-life problems and illustrations often put students in the role of practicing attorneys, real-life exercises are frequently highly engaging and motivating.

A number of excellent resources can give you specific ideas for making experiential teaching and learning courses effective and for including experiential exercises in a large range of law school courses. We encourage you to talk to your colleagues at your school and other institutions. In addition, law school specific resources include:

- Maranville, Bliss, Kaas & López, Building on Best Practices: Transforming Legal Education in a Changing World (Lexis-Nexis 2015).

- Wortham, Scherr, Maurer & Brooks, Learning from Practice: A Text for Experiential Legal Education (3d ed., West 2016).
- Grant, Simpson & Terry, Experiential Education in the Law School Curriculum (Carolina Academic Press, forthcoming 2017).
- Hess, Friedland, Sparrow, & Schwartz, Techniques for Teaching Law 2 (Carolina Academic Press 2011).
- Institute for Law Teaching and Learning Website, http://law teaching.org.

Because we believe it is important to incorporate experiential learning throughout the curriculum, this chapter focuses on concrete ways in which to bring real-life experiences into doctrinal courses. We recognize that reading statutes and cases are real-life experiences; in this chapter, we focus on additional exercises to provide depth and breadth to students' learning. This chapter first identifies a number of methods and illustrates them with specific examples from doctrinal courses. It then follows with suggestions about experiential design choices and process.

Experiential Exercises and Methods

We have used and observed colleagues using a wide variety of experiential exercises lasting as short as a few minutes or as long as an entire semester. We recommend that you be intentional about incorporating experiential exercises in class, start slow and small, reflect upon the experience, and adjust over time to improve students' learning. Illustration 7-1 identifies a variety of experiential or real-life methods to use in a doctrinal course, and suggests how students might engage with those methods. More details about each of these methods and examples of how they can be used in doctrinal courses follows Illustration 7-1.

Illustration 7-1. Some Experiential Methods Appropriate for Doctrinal Courses

Experiential Methods		
	Experiential Methods	Possibilities for Student Engagement
1.	**Current Events and Real-life Stories** — news stories, examples from practice, videos, photos	Research, read and view, report to class, connect to doctrine
2.	**Documents** — claims, contracts or contract clauses, forms, letters, pleadings, trusts, etc.	Read, review, analyze, comment upon, apply to rules
3.	**Drafting Documents** or parts of documents — public comments, code proposals, letters, opinion pieces, emails, questions, etc.	Outline, draft, revise, self- and peer-critique, respond to
4.	**Field Trips** — agency hearings, legislative sessions, courts, medical examiner, construction sites, neighborhoods, prisons, hospitals, etc.	Develop questions, attend, observe, ask questions, photograph, videotape, summarize and share information
5.	**Guest Speakers** — potential clients, experts, lawyers, adjudicators	Develop questions, attend, ask questions, summarize and share information
6.	**Interviews** — potential clients, lawyers, legal constituents, legislators, regulators, judges, engineers, social workers, etc.	Research, develop questions, conduct interview, summarize and share information learned
7.	**Problem-solving** — current or realistic problems facing lawyers and clients	Research, develop questions, collaborate with practitioners; prepare, generate and present alternative solutions
8.	**Short Role Plays** — advocating, negotiating, interviewing, counseling, etc.	Practice being attorneys or clients in short problems

Illustration 7-1. Some Experiential Methods Appropriate for Doctrinal Courses, *continued*

	Experiential Methods	Possibilities for Student Engagement
9.	**Simulations** — more complex role plays	Prepare and explain material to clients and constituents, advise supervisors, negotiate agreements, gather and respond to new information, practice research and writing under time constraints
10.	**Student presentations** — informing, explaining, advocating, demonstrating lawyering skills in front of others	Prepare, practice and engage in giving presentation with audience; provide feedback to peers; role-play decision-makers and other constituents

Specific Examples of Experiential Exercises

Note that the same experiential method or experience can be used for multiple purposes in multiple ways. Students could read an actual contract as an example of what one might look like, revise and edit the contract to improve it, draft an additional provision, role-play different sides in negotiating the contract and its enforcement provisions, draft a client letter explaining certain provisions in the contract, or draft a client letter about the contract's validity and purpose.

1. Current Events and Real-Life Stories

Having students or teachers bring in current events helps students connect more abstract doctrine to real-life events, and shows them how the doctrinal topic is relevant. Real life examples can provide new insight about concepts and stimulate discussion.

Reading or listening to the news, creating media alerts for new developments in particular topics, and asking colleagues and practitioners about current events can be a quick, easy and low-cost way to incorporate real life into your course.

Examples of Current Events and Real-Life Stories

- In a professional responsibility course, the teacher reads the names of the attorneys disciplined by the state bar for violating the principles the class is studying that day.
- Students each research and bring in a news story case decided within the past five years that addresses portions of a criminal law, administrative, tax, or other course.
- A teacher relates course material to what the teacher, a colleague, or a former student actually did in practice.
- Students discuss how doctrine will affect current issues such as transgender access to single-sex schools and public bathrooms.

2. Documents — Reading and Reviewing

Students are often fascinated to see real-life documents related to course material. Real-life documents provide a context and experience different from reading about a document in a case. Even when students have been exposed to legal documents in their lives, such as with credit card agreements, making the connection between those documents and their contracts or consumer protection law course material helps them see their own documents and the course material in a new light.

Examples of Using Real-Life Documents

- Torts students analyze and critique releases signed by members at a local fitness center. (This exercise is also an example of a current event, and could include a field trip.)
- A contracts teacher shows the rock group Van Halen's "no m&m" contract with concert venues; another teacher shows the Harry Potter book contracts.

- Students bring in their credit card agreements, automobile insurance policies, and apartment leases, applying relevant doctrine to analyze the provisions.
- Students read actual complaints, discovery documents, deeds, wills, trusts, security disclosures, environmental impact statements, and other documents frequently prepared and analyzed by lawyers in particular disciplines.

3. Documents—Drafting

Students learn material in a different way when they have to draft a document or portion of a document themselves. Drafting a document requires them to apply legal doctrines to facts using precise and organized written prose. This requires more sophisticated analysis and application skills than responding verbally to a hypothetical problem.

Examples of Document Drafting Exercises

- Students make written public comments on a proposed current federal environmental regulation. (For details about this exercise, see Appendix 8-2.)
- In groups, students prepare a short email to a public employer about reading employees' private emails.
- Students individually draft a cease and desist letter or a potential trademark client.
- Students representing a mentally-disabled borrower prepare mediation summaries for a dispute about an automobile loan.
- Students write and submit opinion pieces about local tribes' access to health care.
- Students draft basic estate documents, such as wills or advance directives, for each other.

4. Field Trips

Students often report that field trips stand out as some of the most memorable learning moments in a course. Field trips connect real-life to doctrine and provide students with a much richer context for legal problems. Students are exposed to things like the setting of a business, the smell of a police station, the slow pace of board hearings, and the wide variety of judging and lawyering styles on display in courts. Field trips can also show students clients' settings and environments.

Field Trip Examples

- At the morgue, students and teacher observe an autopsy of a crime victim.
- Students attend meetings of the international trade law section of the state bar association.
- Health law students visit the local hospital's emergency room on a weekend evening.
- Poverty law students visit and volunteer at a local food bank.
- Education law students attend a school board meeting.

One of the best way to make sure students engage deeply in field trip experiences is to require students to write reflective essays about their experiences. Appendix 7-1 includes an example of a post-field trip reflective essay assignment.

5. Guest Speakers

Students appreciate hearing from speakers who have relevant real-life experience in the field and can relate course principles to law practice. Often the same message given by a teacher resonates significantly more with students when delivered by a guest speaker.

Examples of Using Guest Speakers

- A prosecutor, defense attorney, and probation officer discuss common challenges and joys of working in the criminal justice system.
- A civil legal aid attorney speaks to remedies students about representing very low income disabled clients in a health care class action.
- In intellectual property, an economist talks to students about valuing clients' intellectual property portfolios.

- An architect speaks to a construction law class about how the Americans with Disabilities Act affects building design.
- The deputy commissioner of the state public utilities commission speaks to land use students about wind turbines.
- A panel of clients speaks to a client counseling and interviewing class to provide the clients' perspective on attorney-client communications.

6. Interviews

Interviews provide students with opportunities to focus research on a topic or person, prepare thoughtful questions, uncover material not included in course materials, and practice summarizing information gained from conversations. Moreover, interviews give students the opportunity to practice interviewing and relational skills, forge relationships, make professional connections, and develop confidence.

Interview Examples

- Students are assigned to interview an attorney in the attorney's office about the attorney's career path, challenges, and successes. (For specifics on this exercise, see Appendix 7-2.)
- A mock client (an actor, student, colleague) comes to a required first-year class and is interviewed by students who have prepared questions in advance.
- In class, employment law students interview in-house counsel about Family Medical Leave Act policies.
- Students interview a child psychiatrist about a child's learning disabilities in preparing for a simulated school individual education program team meeting.
- In an admiralty law class, students interview officials from the Harbor Department's legal problems with container ships.

7. Problem-Solving

Students are usually motivated to learn when they are asked to consider complex scenarios and shape a variety of solutions based on real-life challenges lawyers face. Students also tend to remember and internalize important knowledge when they have to apply strategies to solve real-life problems. In addition, asking students to solve problems in groups promotes collaboration, teamwork, diversity, and respect.

Examples of Student Problem-Solving

- Working in groups, students research and prepare a one-page email about the carbon monoxide dangers of a specific waterski boat model, and advise a mock supervisor whether they have sufficient information to bring a products liability defective warning claim against the manufacturer. Students also conduct factual research about the dangers of the boat design and the properties of carbon monoxide poisoning. (For specifics on this exercise, see Appendix 7-3.)
- Given facts about a private nuisance affecting a residential homeowner and given a mock client's goals, remedies students make brief presentations to classmates and the teacher about the various possible remedies
- Tax students analyze and explain the tax consequences for TV show winners of Oprah Winfrey's "You Get a Car!" program.
- Given a mock client's wishes about distributing her assets upon death, trusts and estate students compare the advantages and disadvantages of using a trust or will. Students also advise the client about the consequences of failing to create any trust or will documents.

8. Short Role Plays

In playing a role, students tend to become more involved in an exercise. They can practice a wide variety of skills, focus on particular skills in isolation, make mistakes in a safer environment than in the workplace, and develop a great appreciation for different points of view, particularly if they role-play a position with which they would otherwise disagree.

Short Role Play Examples

- Taking turns playing the role of attorney and client, pairs of students spend ten minutes conducting initial interviews of an employer and employee client engaged in a labor dispute.
- Pairs of criminal law students act as prosecutors and defense attorneys in negotiating a plea agreement.
- Two students advise a third student about an entertainment law dispute.
- In the role of agency officials, sports law students explain decisions and reasoning about a doping complaint filed against an athlete.
- Evidence students argue motions advocating for and against suppressing medical records.
- Gender and the law students put themselves in the role of managers teaching employees about sexual harassment.
- Students in election law represent different constituents in a redistricting hearing.

9. Simulations

More complex than simple role-plays, simulations typically engage students in a variety of other experiential methods, such as reading and drafting documents, conducting interviews, role-playing, problem-solving, and presenting information. Some teachers engage students in semester-long simulations during which students experience a wide range of challenges lawyers encounter in practice. Other teachers have students engage in shorter simulations, such as drafting and negotiating a contract, making oral arguments, making a presentation for a simulated client, or conducting a mock client interview.

Example of Simulation with Multiple Steps

(See Appendix 7-4 for another example.)

- Students are provided with a few basic facts about a mock military client facing a court-martial for sexual harassment.

- Before interviewing the client, a librarian gives a short in-class presentation about practice-based resources related to military justice. For homework, students conduct outside research and prepare interview questions.
- In class, small groups of students compare their research findings and brainstorm the most important questions to ask the client.
- Students next take turns interviewing the client in class to learn more about the client's circumstances and goals.
- Reconvening in small groups, students compare and analyze the client's facts and goals, and prepare to advise the client.
- Following a class in which a few students take turns advising the client, all students are put in the role of the military prosecutor and assigned to prepare arguments against the client.
- In the final simulation of the experiential module, students play the roles of the client, client advocate, witnesses, military prosecutor, and administrative discharge board officials.
- At the end of the simulation, students write reflective papers responding to specific prompts about their experience in the different roles.

10. Student Presentations

When students have to make presentations in front of the whole or part of a class, they often perform at a higher level than when asked to present to the teacher alone. Moreover, the choice to trust students as "teachers" communicates a high level of confidence in students' abilities.

Examples of Student Presentations

- Students prepare concept maps about significant art law topics, show images to class, explain and respond to questions.
- Choosing individual privacy law topics, students research and prepare short lectures to class.

- Groups of students engage their classmates in an interactive ten-minute lesson about current events tied to the day's reading assignments.
- In class, an individual student presents a real and fictional current event on climate change, challenging the class to identify which is which.
- Small groups of students design hypotheticals which they pose to their classmates and then analyze for the class.

Designing Experiential Exercises and Methods

We recommend that you consider the design considerations below, and we encourage you to use your own approach and sequence in developing exercises and using experiential methods. Bear in mind that the way you expect an exercise to work may be very different from what actually happens for students.

Considerations for Designing Experiential Exercises

1. Learning goal/s and objective/s
2. Experiential method/s (see Illustration 7-1)
3. Overall structure
4. Relevant and significant material
5. Clear goals, directions, and expectations
6. Teacher preparation
7. Student preparation
8. Feedback
9. Reflection for students
10. Reflection and self-assessment for teacher

1. Focus on Learning Goals and Objectives

As with other aspects of course and class design (see Chapters 3 and 4), connect experiential exercises and methods with your course learning goals. In general, the more time the experiential exercise takes, the closer it should relate to important learning goals. Having students participate in a simulation may be motivating and engaging for its own sake, but relating real-life exercises to important course learning goals is more likely to produce significant learning.

2. Choose the Experiential Method/s

Illustration 7-1 and the more detailed descriptions above and in the appendix suggest ways to infuse real-life experiences in a doctrinal course. If you are new to experiential teaching, you may want to start by using an exercise that seems most compatible with your teaching approach. Because experiential exercises may invite new teaching challenges and surprises, we recommend you begin with a method that feels comfortable. Experiential learning exercises require the teacher to relinquish some control over the class, and it is often difficult to predict how long an effective exercise should last. It's usually easier to design an experiential exercise when you adapt one a colleague has already designed. Tweaking those exercises and making them fit your course goals and students may be more efficient than designing one completely on your own.

3. Design the Overall Structure

Once you have identified why you want students to have a real-life exercise and what method(s) you want to use, consider specifically what you want students to do and when. To understand easements, property students could take a photo of an easement after they have learned about them and post it to a course website. Or they could be asked to research a city's housing and zoning laws and canvas a neighborhood to determine how certain property laws appear to affect its composition mid-semester. Several weeks into a patent law course, students could attempt to draft claims for a new pizza box design. At the beginning of the term, immigration law students could complete a citizenship test, later draft immigration forms, and toward the end of the semester take a field trip to observe an immigration detention facility. Scheduled throughout the term, criminal law students could accompany police officers on their beats. Constitutional law students could listen to Supreme Court oral arguments and read parties' and amicus briefs on topics related to those they are currently learning about. Tax students could be asked to summarize a current tax problem related to the material they are studying in the course and orally present it and answer questions about it from a simulated client or supervising attorney.

4. Find Relevant and Significant Material

Students are more likely to be engaged in real-life exercises that seem important and relevant to the topic. For example, because most negligence cases are settled before trial, it may be more effective to have torts students prepare a demand letter or settlement proposal to a defendant's insurance company rather than prepare closing arguments for a trial.

Practicing attorneys, former students, colleagues, recent cases, continuing legal education materials, bar journal articles, and scholarly articles can be useful sources for real-life exercises. Letting students know that the role-play you assigned was based on an actual matter helps the students put themselves in the role of lawyers and connect course knowledge and skills to the problems.

5. Provide Clear Goals, Directions, and Expectations

Be clear about what you expect students to do and what the results of the real-world exercise should look like. It's much more effective to direct students to spend an hour researching facts related to a product's defective design than it is to ask them to just "research facts." Explain what the result of students' work should be, such as "by the end of class, each group must post a one-page document listing the two most significant remedies available for the breach of the building sale contract and the main reasons why those remedies are most important."

Upper-level courses, in which students can be expected to have greater knowledge and skills and are closer to practicing law, might call for less explicit instructions and more complex problems. For example, an insurance law teacher might assign students to write a client advice letter about the various insurance options available to the client. The teacher's instructions could be that the students need to find and evaluate the options, explain what the client needs to have explained, and write a letter "long enough to appropriately convey the important information using words the client can understand." For such assignments, it helps to provide directions and guidance consistent with what students might experience in a summer internship or initial job as an attorney.

To write clear directions, work backwards from what you want students to accomplish. Break down the different steps so that students can be successful. For example, if you want students to all spend about 15 minutes engaged in a paired role-play where one student attorney advises another student playing the role of a bankrupt and suicidal client, you should provide students in the different roles with different directions, specify how the students are to behave, and explain what they are to accomplish by the end of the role-play.

In designing an experiential exercise that lasts more than a few minutes, it helps to follow the principles of designing active learning activities (see Chapter 6) and assessment (see Chapter 9). Put the goals, directions and performance expectations in writing and have someone else—assistant, teaching fellow, colleague or friend—read the material and see if that person understands what you have written and knows what he or she would need to do.

6. Identify What You Have to Do to Adequately Prepare for the Exercise

Are there special materials needed? Do you need to find a different classroom with flexible seating? How much research should you do? How will you connect this exercise to the course material? Depending on the complexity of the exercise and other teaching methods used in the course, consider what additional preparation you will need to do and how much time you should allocate for it.

7. Identify What Students Have to Do to Adequately Prepare for the Exercise

If the experiential exercise you choose requires you to bring in current events related to your course everyday, students may have no additional preparation. If, however, you want students to actively engage in the exercise, such as listening to a guest speaker, having them prepare for the exercise leads to higher engagement. For example, rather than have students sit through a hospital risk management attorney's guest lecture about health law, have students research her and bring questions to class for the attorney. Prepared students bring more depth and sophistication to real-life experiences so consider what will best help students be effective. Consider too what will happen if students are unprepared or minimally prepared.

8. Determine What Feedback Students Will Receive

Students' performance in an experiential exercise might be graded as a separate assignment, considered as part of a class participation grade, required as part of the course, or completely ungraded. You may decide to provide individual comments, rubrics, group or whole-class feedback, or none. For more ideas about giving feedback, see Chapter 9, Assessing Student Learning.

9. Determine Whether Students Will Reflect Upon the Exercise

One of the hallmarks of effective experiential learning is that students reflect upon their experiences and learn from them. Being self-aware and thoughtful about what they have experienced leads to greater learning gains and maximizes real-life exposure. For longer and more involved experiential exercises, we recommend that you ask students to reflect upon their experience and how they might apply what they have learned to future practice. As is true of all reflection exercises, a more specific set of questions (e.g., What did you observe the lawyer do that surprised you? How will this experience influence you in the future?) is more effective than a prompt to "reflect on your experience." (Examples of reflective prompts are in Appendix 7 and 9.)

10. Reflect and Self-Assess the Experience

Just as students learn from reflecting about their real-life experiences, we recommend that you too consider and write down the features of the experiential exercise that worked well, the parts that went poorly, and where you might make changes in the future. For more on using reflection and teaching journals to improve your teaching and student learning, see Chapter 11, Developing as a Teacher.

Illustration 7-2. Experiential Teaching and Learning Checklist

Experiential Teaching and Learning

❏ **Foundational considerations**
  ❏ Understand the value of experiential teaching and learning to promote deep understanding

❏ **Consider the variety of experiential methods**
  ❏ Current events and real-life stories
  ❏ Documents
  ❏ Drafting
  ❏ Field trips
  ❏ Guest speakers
  ❏ Interviews
  ❏ Problem solving
  ❏ Small role-plays
  ❏ Simulations
  ❏ Student presentations

❏ **Design the experiential exercise**
  ❏ Connect to learning objectives
  ❏ Choose appropriate methods
  ❏ Design overall structure
  ❏ Select relevant and significant material
  ❏ Describe clear goals, directions, and expectations
  ❏ Identify teacher preparation
  ❏ Identify student preparation
  ❏ Determine feedback methods
  ❏ Determine student reflection
  ❏ Reflect and self-assess

You will find examples of the concepts from this chapter in Appendix 7 on the book's website—http://lawteaching.org/resources.

Appendix 7-1: Field Trip Reflective Paper—Criminal Court Observation

Appendix 7-2: Lawyer Interview

Appendix 7-3: Defective Product Exercise

Appendix 7-4: Client Interview and Demand Letter

Additional examples are in

Appendix 5-1: Role Plays

Appendix 5-2: Experiential Professionalism Instruction

Appendix 8-2: Public Comment Assignments and Classes

Chapter 8

Deep, Lasting Learning

What constitutes exceptional, significant learning? How can we foster deep, lasting learning for our students? These are important questions for us as teachers. We all struggle to develop courses and classes that produce profound, persistent learning.

What Is Exceptional, Significant, Lasting Learning?

In the first phase of our research for the book *What the Best Law Teachers Do* (2014), we solicited nominations of law teachers who produced exceptional learning in their students. We invited the nominators to articulate their definitions of exceptional learning. Many of the nominators gave thoughtful examples and explanations of exceptional intellectual and personal development in law school.

Intellectual development begins with a deep, nuanced understanding of core legal concepts and skills. Core concepts include analytical frameworks, underlying theories, and ambiguities in areas of substantive and procedural law. Core skills include legal analysis, legal research, drafting, fact investigation, advocacy, counseling, negotiation, and the development of professional judgment. Successful learners can critically analyze problems, synthesize ideas from different areas of law, and view legal challenges through various perspectives. Ultimately, exceptional intellectual development prepares students to apply concepts and skills in law practice and life after graduation.

Personal development begins with students' self-awareness of their strengths, weaknesses, cognition, assumptions, biases, and emotions. Exceptional personal development can be transformative, building students' confidence, allowing students to achieve personal and professional goals beyond what they thought was possible. Exceptional personal development inspires students to become lifelong learners. Finally, exceptional personal development includes students acquiring the core values of the profession and developing a professional identity based on those values.

As part of our data gathering for *What the Best Law Teachers Do*, we interviewed dozens of current and former students of the twenty-six law teachers we studied in depth. We asked those students and alumni to identify the lasting learning (if any) that they gained from those teachers. The lessons that stuck with them included subject matter, skills, and values.

Some students and alumni identified subject matter that stuck with them. However, they did not focus on discrete rules of law (the elements of battery, hearsay exceptions, the *Erie* doctrine). Rather, their lasting learning included the idea that legal rules are indeterminate and constantly changing. They learned frameworks for analysis to address future problems in an area of law. Their teachers inspired these students to pursue careers in particular fields of law, including election law, immigration law, tax law, and civil rights.

For many students and alumni, the focus of their lasting learning was skills. Students learned transferable analytical skills including close reading of cases and statutes, attention to detail, problem solving, and nuanced analysis of court opinions and statutes. Many alumni noted drafting, writing, and advocacy skills that they learned in law school and currently employ in law practice.

The most common types of lasting learning, by far, concerned personal development, values, and professionalism. Take-away lessons for students and alumni included:

- developing a strong work ethic;
- striving for excellence;
- bringing passion to their work;
- maintaining a balance between confidence and humility;
- treating clients with compassion and humanity;

- being respectful in every interaction with clients, lawyers, judges, staff, witnesses, and everyone else in the profession;
- making conscious choices about their professional identities;
- living healthy, balanced lives;
- exemplifying integrity and responsibility; and
- embracing an ethic of service and a quest for justice.

How Can Teachers Foster Deep, Lasting Learning for Students?

Four principles guide teachers in designing courses to foster deep, lasting learning for students:

1. Choose learning objectives that address significant, lasting learning;
2. Create a challenging, supportive, collaborative teaching and learning environment;
3. Engage students in rich, textured learning activities; and
4. Incorporate frequent formative feedback.

Choose Learning Objectives That Address Significant, Lasting Learning

Identifying learning objectives that address significant, lasting learning is the first step for teachers in designing courses to foster deep learning for students. We cannot overemphasize the importance of this step.

Our conscious decision to choose specific, deep learning objectives for a course has several implications. First, as we discussed in Chapters 3 and 4, the first step in intentional course and class design is to identify learning objectives. Lasting learning should be built into courses and class sessions from the beginning of the design process. Second, most teachers feel pressure to cover large volumes of content in their courses. We believe that foundational content should be included in learning objectives for many courses. But core content objectives should not be the <u>only</u> learning objectives. Instead, courses should also include lasting learning objectives beyond foundational knowledge. Third, we should be thoughtful and selective when choosing lasting learning objectives for our courses. Although there is no "correct" number of lasting learning objectives for a course, we believe that at least three such objectives are appropriate for most courses.

The particular deep learning goals appropriate for a course depend on many variables, including the nature of the course, the students, and the teacher. The following questions address some of the relevant considerations.

- Is the course required? Recommended? Elective?
- Is it a survey course (Evidence)? A specialty course (Transactional Drafting)?
- Is the subject tested on most bar exams?
- Where are the students in their legal education? First-semester, first-year? Second-semester, third-year?
- What background, experience, or prior learning do students bring to the course?
- What types of jobs do most students secure after graduation?
- In what areas does the teacher have the most expertise? Least expertise?
- Which concepts, theories, skills, and values is the teacher particularly passionate about?

After considering the nature of the course, students, and teacher, think expansively about appropriate lasting learning goals for your courses.

- In your wildest dreams, what learning would students take away from your course?
- What learning do you hope persists after students graduate?
- What learning would most help students in their professional lives? In their personal lives?

There are hundreds, perhaps thousands, of lasting learning objectives appropriate for law school courses. When making choices about significant, deep learning objectives for a particular course, it may help to categorize those objectives into (1) knowledge and analytical skills, (2) practice and relational skills, (3) professionalism, values, and identity. For each of the three categories, Illustration 8-1 lists many subcategories and several examples of lasting learning objectives.

Illustration 8-1. Lasting Learning Objectives

Categories and Subcategories	Sample Learning Objectives
Knowledge and Analytical Skills Analytical frameworks Underlying policies Theoretical approaches Legal analysis (IRAC) Legal argument Case analysis Statutory analysis Constitutional interpretation Critical thinking Creative thinking Problem solving Close reading Attention to detail	Students will be able to: • Develop an analytical framework for an area of law relevant to a client's problem • Use underlying policies and theory to support arguments on behalf of a client • Generate multiple reasonable approaches to help achieve a client's goals
Practice and Relational Skills Legal research Written communication Oral communication Listening Legal drafting Fact investigation Interviewing & Questioning Negotiating Counselling Trial advocacy Practical judgment Organizing & managing projects Leadership Teamwork Cultural competence	Students will be able to: • Efficiently find applicable cases, statutes, and regulations relevant to a client's problem • Employ applicable negotiation styles and strategies to resolve a dispute • Build cross-cultural skills by practicing habits of cross-cultural lawyering

Illustration 8-1. Lasting Learning Objectives, *cont.*

Categories and Subcategories	Sample Learning Objectives
Professionalism, Values, and Identity Honesty & integrity Self-motivation & diligence Reliability & responsibility Seeking fairness & justice Passion & respect Balance & stress-management Self-confidence & humility Empathy & tolerance Commitment to *pro bono* & social justice Self-reflection	Students will: • Always show respect for clients, lawyers, judges, staff, witnesses, etc. • Engage in self-reflection to continuously improve as professionals • Incorporate *pro bono* as a significant aspect of their professional lives

Create a Challenging, Supportive, Collaborative Teaching and Learning Environment

Students' motivation directly affects the depth and persistence of their learning. Student motivation tends to be highest in a teaching and learning environment that is challenging, supportive, and collaborative.

A challenging learning environment begins with clear expectations that students will achieve deep, lasting learning goals. A teacher's high expectations can have dramatic effects on students' preparation and performance. High expectations are essential to an effective teaching and learning environment. But high expectations alone are not enough. Students will be more motivated to excel when they perceive that the teacher's expectations for lasting learning are both high and achievable. In other words, student motivation increases when they believe that what they are learning is meaningful, that their teachers expect a lot from them, and that they can succeed if they work hard. It is important for teachers to communicate high expectations for every student in the course along with the belief that every student can succeed. These uniform expectations and confidence that each student can achieve great things can be powerful motivators for students. Students respond to teachers who model high expectations. Teachers who demonstrate high expectations for their own performance inspire students to achieve important lasting learning goals.

Most students excel in teaching and learning environments that are not only challenging but supportive as well. A fundamental characteristic of a supportive environment is mutual respect between students and teachers. Other teachers' attitudes that lead to a supportive teaching and learning environment include caring deeply about student learning, concern for students' well-being in and out of the classroom, and confidence in every student's promise and potential.

"Collaborative" is a third attribute of a teaching and learning environment that fosters deep, lasting learning. Most of the outstanding law teachers we studied view their relationship with students as collaborative rather than hierarchical. They see their students as colleagues and peers. They treat students as adults and professionals. Their students notice and appreciate this collaborative environment.

Engage Students in Rich, Textured Learning Activities

Students are more likely to achieve significant, lasting learning if they engage in learning activities that are rich and textured.

Our conception of rich learning activities, which we adapt from L. Dee Fink, *Creating Significant Learning Experiences* (2013), has three phases: (1) students encounter important content; (2) students actively engage with the content; and (3) students reflect on their learning. Each of these phases could take place outside of class, in an on-line class, or in a face-to-face class.

In Phase 1, students encounter important content, which could include ideas, principles, policies, theories, perspectives, values, strategies, etc. Content could address learning objectives related to knowledge, skills, or values. Students can encounter content in many different ways. Students could read cases, statutes, articles, or stories. Students could view videos, pictures, diagrams, or demonstrations. Students could listen to lectures, presentations, or podcasts.

Illustration 8-2. Rich Learning Activities

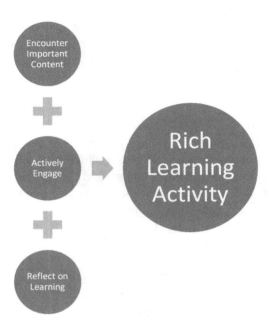

In Phase 2, students work with the content by engaging in active learning activities. Students ask and respond to questions, produce outlines and diagrams, participate in discussions and debates, analyze hypotheticals and problems, make arguments orally and in writing, draft transactional and litigation documents, conduct fact investigations and discovery, interview and counsel simulated or real clients. These examples just scratch the surface of potential active learning methods. Other examples appear throughout the book. Students can engage in active learning individually, in small groups, or in a large group.

In Phase 3, students reflect on their learning. Reflection solidifies learning for students. For example, students can complete a "minute paper" at the end of a class session in which they articulate a key lesson from the class—"Explain the policies that underlie attorney-client privilege." (See the discussion of minute papers in Chapter 9.) Reflection can help students identify strengths and weaknesses in their performance after a mid-term exam, a draft of a paper, or a witness interview. And reflection can help students think through how to improve their understanding and performance in the future. (See Chapter 5 and Appendix 5 for examples of reflection activities, including reflective writing.)

Our conception of textured learning activities has three components: multiple, varied, and progressive.

Illustration 8-3. Textured Learning Activities

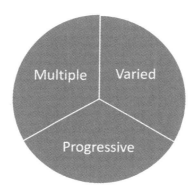

In the context of textured learning activities, multiple means that students will encounter and work with the relevant concept or skill or value more than once in the course. The more important the learning objective, the more learning experiences directed at the objective the students should have throughout the course. Varied means that the students will employ more than one type of learning activity directed at the objective. For example, students may read a rule of evidence, discuss a case interpreting the rule, work on problems applying the rule with a small group of students, see a demonstration of a lawyer employing the rule in offering evidence, and participate in a simulation in which the student argues about the admissibility of evidence under the rule. Progressive means that the difficulty of the issues and level of sophistication of students' performance grows during the course. For example, first students read an article about a jurisprudential theory to try to understand it, then they attempt to explain how the theory plays out in a judicial opinion, then they compare it to other theories, then they make a written argument employing the theory, then they critique and revise the theory.

The examples below, Illustrations 8-4 and 8-5, illustrate rich, textured learning activities.

Illustration 8-4. Statutory Analysis Example

Context. Statutory analysis skills could be an important objective of any course in which statutes provide a significant part of the applicable law.

Objective. Students will be able to use the elements of statutory analysis to make effective arguments in this course and in practice.

Learning Activities:
- Introductory lecture. Emphasize the importance of statutory analysis skills to succeed in the course and in practice. Define six elements of statutory analysis: (1) language of the applicable statute, (2) purpose of the statute, (3) overall statutory scheme, (4) legislative history, (5) regulations interpreting the statute, and (6) cases interpreting the statute.
- Teacher demonstrates the six elements in analyzing a simple problem.
- Throughout the course, reading assignments ask students to identify judges' use of statutory analysis in opinions followed by in-class Socratic dialog or large group discussion of the opinions.
- Multiple assignments asking students to use elements of statutory analysis to prepare arguments based on relatively simple problems, followed by small and large group discussion of the problems in class.
- Students complete a minute paper reflecting on their statutory analysis strengths and weaknesses at the end of a class in which students work on problems.
- Students complete a practice exam asking them to use the elements of statutory analysis to make an argument in a complex problem.
- Large group discussion in class of a rubric or score sheet for the practice exam problem, followed by student reflection on strengths and weaknesses of their performance.
- A substantial portion of the final exam incudes an essay question that requires students to use the elements of statutory analysis to make an argument in a complex problem.

Illustration 8-5. Public Comment Example

Context. The public comment process could be an important objective in any course with a substantial component of administrative law.

Objective. For the public comment process on proposed agency action, students will be able to (1) articulate the purpose and requirements of the process (2) critique the process, and (3) identify characteristics of effective public comments.

Learning Activities:
- Reading assignment with statutory provisions, agency regulations, and cases addressing the purposes and requirements of the opportunity for public comment on proposed agency actions.
- Assignment for students to review a sampling of public comments (posted on the course webpage).
- Large group discussion in class of the purpose, requirements, strengths and weaknesses of the public comment process.
- Assignment requiring each student to write and file a written public comment on a pending administrative agency action.
- Assignment that each student post on the course web page the text of the public comment that they made and a paragraph reflecting on what the student learned from participating in the public comment process.
- Assignment that each student reviews two of their fellow students' postings.
- Large group discussion in class regarding the purposes of the public comment process, the strengths and weaknesses of the process, and characteristics of effective public comments.

Appendix 8-1 is a more detailed description of public comment assignments and class sessions.

Incorporate Frequent Formative Feedback

Feedback is central to learning. Frequent, formative feedback furthers student achievement of significant, lasting learning goals. We address feedback throughout this book: Chapter 4 (the role of feedback in class design); Chapter 5 (feedback through students' self-reflection); and Chapter 9 (a detailed exploration of assessing students to improve their learning). Rather than repeating that discussion here, we apply formative feedback principles to our two examples of rich, textured learning experiences.

Rich, textured learning activities offer many opportunities for formative feedback. Sources of feedback include the teacher, other students, and the student herself. Feedback can occur in and outside of class. Feedback can be delivered in a large group setting, to small groups of students, or one-on-one to an individual student.

Statutory Analysis Example (Illustration 8-4) — Formative Feedback.

- Assignments throughout the course ask students to identify judges' use of statutory analysis elements in opinions and to prepare statutory analysis arguments in response to short problems. Large and small group discussions of these assignments in class give students feedback on their ability to identify elements and make arguments.
- In the minute paper, students give themselves feedback on their statutory analysis strengths and weaknesses.
- The practice exam exercise allows for several feedback options:
  ◦ Teacher could make comments on each student's response;
  ◦ Teacher could complete a score sheet or rubric evaluating each student's response;
  ◦ Teacher could prepare a score sheet or rubric and have students apply it to their own responses or to another student's response;
  ◦ Teacher could prepare a score sheet or rubric and conduct a large group discussion in class;
  ◦ Teacher could meet individually with any student who wants more feedback.
- The final exam also offers multiple opportunities for formative feedback:
  ◦ Students can review the teacher's comments on their responses;

- ° Students can review the score sheet or rubric completed by the teacher;
- ° Teacher could prepare a memo to students summarizing common strengths and weaknesses in student responses;
- ° Teacher could meet individually with any student who wants more feedback.

Public Comment Example (Illustration 8-5) — Formative Feedback.

The assignment that each student make a public comment on a proposed agency action and post the text of the comment on the course website allows for several types of formative feedback:

- Students could engage in self feedback by posting a paragraph reflecting on what the student learned from participating in the public comment process;
- Students could provide feedback to one another by posting reactions and questions to one-another's public comments;
- Teacher could post a paragraph of feedback on each student's public comment;
- Teacher could prepare a memo to students summarizing the themes that emerged from the students' public comments and the students' reflections on their learning.

Illustration 8-6 is a checklist for fostering deep, lasting student learning.

Illustration 8-6. Fostering Deep, Lasting Learning Checklist

Fostering Deep, Lasting Learning

❏ **Foundational considerations:**
- ❏ Articulate your view of what constitutes exceptional learning in law school
- ❏ Articulate your vision of learning that your students retain after graduation

❏ **Choose learning objectives that address significant, lasting learning**
- ❏ Knowledge and analytical skills
- ❏ Practice and relational skills
- ❏ Professionalism, values, and identity

❏ **Create an effective teaching and learning environment**
- ❏ Challenging
- ❏ Supportive
- ❏ Collaborative

❏ **Engage students in rich, textured learning activities**
- ❏ Rich
- ❏ Students encounter important content (knowledge, skills, values)
- ❏ Students actively engage with the content
- ❏ Students reflect on their learning
- ❏ Textured
- ❏ Multiple
- ❏ Varied
- ❏ Progressive

❏ **Incorporate frequent formative feedback**
- ❏ Feedback from teacher
- ❏ Feedback from other students
- ❏ Self feedback

Chapter 9

Assessing Student Learning

Introduction

In this chapter, we focus on designing effective assessment approaches and instruments, both to give you and the students feedback during the course and to assign grades.

Illustration 9-1 identifies the steps essential to any assessment process.

Illustration 9-1. Designing Effective Assessments — 3 Steps

1. Identify what you want to assess (learning objectives)
2. Prepare and give assessment instruments
3. Give feedback to students

Step One: Identify Learning Objectives

Learning objectives should articulate the knowledge, skills, and values you expect students to learn in the course. If you are unsure about your learning objectives, consider what you expect students to do well in the course. The kinds of intellectual skills and knowledge you test on the final exam are good indicators of what you want students to learn in the course. For further guidance, look at the examples of course goals and objectives in Chapters 3 and 4.

Step Two: Prepare the Assessment Instrument

There are many different kinds of assessment instruments you can use in law school. Illustration 9-2 includes some of these.

Illustration 9-2. Assessment Instruments

1. Multiple-choice and short answer quizzes
2. Analytical, issue-spotting, and advocacy essays
3. Outlines, charts and matrices
4. Legal documents such as wills, articles of incorporation, injunctions, statutes
5. Journals
6. Role-plays—simulations with students engaged in practice-related performances
7. Verbal presentations and oral arguments
8. Skits, movies, games, artwork, ... and on and on.

Regardless of the kind of assessment you are doing, as you prepare the instrument, consider the factors described below and listed in Illustration 9-3.

Illustration 9-3. Factors to Consider When Preparing Assessment Instruments

- What is the rationale for this assessment?
- What do you want students to do?
- What is the assessment's content?
- How will you provide feedback?

By answering these questions, you can prevent a lot of wasted time and effort—yours and the students'.

Provide the Rationale for the Assessment

Make sure your students know *why* you are asking them to perform the assessment and what feedback they can expect. For example:

> *Let's figure out how this rule applies. I'm giving you some facts and am asking you to make a decision. After you make your decisions, we'll discuss some valid responses. This interaction will give you practice and verbal feedback on applying this rule.*

Be Explicit about What Students Should Do

Provide ultra-precise and clear directions. Give students plenty of white space, use bullets, numbers, and different forms of emphasis to help them stay on task. Write all directions in plain English, using sentences of 25 words or less and paragraphs of 4–8 sentences. Unless you intend an ambiguity, there should no doubt about what students are expected to do.

If possible, give students the directions before a graded assessment. It can reduce needless stress if students know what they will be expected to do and are aware of the exam's format, number of questions and time allotted.

Ask specific questions, such as, "Is this a valid trust? Why or why not?" rather than "Discuss plaintiff's claims." Similarly, when presenting a hypothetical problem, be clear about whether students should be selective about what facts they apply or identify as many as possible. In addition consider telling students what *not* do. For example: "Please focus on the problematic aspects of the articles of incorporation. **Do not** discuss the provisions that are clear." **If at all possible, do the assessment yourself, revising it based on what you want to emphasize.**

Tell students how much time they have to complete the assessment. Students will usually take twice as much time as you would to complete an assessment. If you don't have the time to do the assessment yourself, see how long it takes to prepare your outline.

Ask a colleague to track how long it took just to read the assessment. Provide sufficient time in or out of class to allow well-prepared students to complete the assessment. If the graded assessment has time constraints, suggest amounts of time for each section as students have a hard time budgeting their time.

Direct students about any particular format or approach they should use, especially if the assessment is graded. How many minutes should their presentations be? Can they use props in their simulations? Should they dress up? Are they expected to speak loudly enough to be heard at the back of the room? Do you have preferences about margins, font type and size, page length, spacing and organizational structure? Alternatively, you may want to leave the options wide open to allow for a greater range of student creativity.

To maximize the benefits of collaboration, some assessments can be group projects, and some a hybrid, such as asking students to prepare an assessment individually and then collaborate with others who have similarly prepared. Another possibility is to have students take an assessment individually but to award a bonus to all the members of a group if everyone in the group performs at or above a predetermined level, such as 80% correct.

Determine the Content of the Assessment

Keeping your learning goals in mind, focus assessments on the most important skills, content, and values in the course. During the course, give students practice integrating different areas by embedding material from an earlier section of the course in a new assessment.

Designing fact patterns or hypotheticals. Consult casebooks, court opinions, restatements, journals, and current events for ideas about realistic scenarios.

Omit distractions that could impede students' learning. For example, using a rape scenario on a criminal exam may provoke powerfully negative emotional responses in students who have been sexually assaulted. Avoid using unexplained references or making assumptions about students' cultural experiences or background knowledge. For example, omit sports references or names of TV shows that may be meaningless to some students.

Keep names simple. Give every person in an assessment a different sounding name. Using one-syllable names that start with "P" or "D" makes it clear who the plaintiffs and defendants are. Include realistic names of corporations, towns, and statutes, such as "Chemical Co." rather than "Big Bad Corp."

Consider including a visual. A photo, a map or other visual can help students more quickly understand the scenario you want them to analyze.

Avoid humor on graded assessments; students do not find graded assessments funny.

Determine How You Will Provide Students with Feedback

You could give "global feedback" where you review all assessments and then provide comments on common themes. You can select excerpts from a few sample assessments and comment on the common strengths and weaknesses. You can also provide a sample answer that students can compare with their written submissions. Students could review and comment upon their peers' work. You can provide a checklist or rubric students can use to self-assess. (More on rubrics below). If you're new at providing feedback, you may want to tell students that you will provide feedback and will determine the particular method after you've seen their work.

Step Three: Give Feedback to Students

The most effective feedback is:

1. **Specific**—information about specific criteria students have or have not met.
2. **Positive**—students find out what they are doing well.
3. **Corrective**—students learn about their weaknesses and get strategies to improve them.
4. **Prompt**—students get feedback while the assessment is fresh and before the next one.

Provide Students with Specific Feedback

Focus on one to three key components that could be improved. One way to give feedback is to first take the assessment yourself, analyze your response, and then make a list of specific things you wanted students to show on this assessment. Use the list to work through student assessments, putting a "check," "check plus," or "check minus" on their work and returning them to students in the next class.

You also can give specific feedback verbally in class, such as by saying,

> *"Excellent! Jana named some critical facts in applying this rule. Each fact helps show why the plaintiff lost. In practice it's essential to show **how** the facts apply to the law."*

Another way to provide specific feedback is to give students a rubric—a grid with a set of detailed written criteria used to assess student performance. Illustration 9-4 shows a sample rubric from a criminal procedure course. Students and teachers can assess performance more effectively when they have a rubric describing specific criteria and levels of quality.

Provide Students with Positive Feedback

Most students learn more effectively when they are validated for what they do well. Give positive feedback at the beginning, even if all you can say is "Nice job using the accurate regulations," to help them build on their successes.

Give Students Feedback about Their Weaknesses and Provide Strategies to Improve Them

- Be direct but compassionate;
- Sandwich specific corrective feedback in between positive feedback;
- Focus on the work, not the person;
- Avoid making normative judgments; and
- Provide strategies to improve.

Illustration 9-4. Sample Rubric

The categories to the right do not necessarily correlate with end of semester grades. → **Description of what is being assessed** ↓	Levels of quality		
	Exemplary	Competent	Developing
Identifies basic and complex criminal procedural issues — "Issue Spotting" 40%	❏ Accurately identifies *all* basic procedural issues *21–30 points* ❏ Identifies *most* of the complex issues *7–10 points*	❏ Accurately identifies *most* basic procedural issues *11–20 points* ❏ Identifies *some* of the more complex issues *4–6 points*	❏ Accurately identifies *some* basic procedural issues *0–10 points* ❏ Identifies a *few* of the more complex issues *0–3 points*
Analyzes the facts 40%	❏ Accurately and explicitly shows how the law applies to important facts *27–40 points*	❏ Accurately shows how the law applies to most of the relevant facts *14–26 points*	❏ Accurately but minimally shows how the law applies to some of the facts *0–13 points*
Identifies and applies the policy for the rules of criminal procedure 20%	❏ Identifies and applies competing policy goals to facts in predicting results *14–20 points*	❏ Somewhat identifies and applies policy to facts in predicting results *7–13 points*	❏ Minimally identifies and applies policy to facts in predicting results *0–6 points*

Examples: *"Your mock client interview would have been more effective if you had stated your advice in simpler language."*

"Great mistake! This document includes exactly what was asked for—factual inferences. Now consider which inferences are reasonable; how might you explain them to a lay person?"

Avoid Making Assumptions

You may assume a student's poor performance shows a lack of effort. Instead, the student may have been facing a crisis or need additional coaching. It also is possible your directions were unclear. But do tell students when their work suggests that they may fail the course. It's a hard message to deliver and to receive, but the message will be even more painful if the student earns the D or F in the course.

Give Students Prompt Feedback

The shorter the assessment, and the fewer the students, the sooner students should receive feedback. Give feedback on a short in-class quiz or hypothetical during that class or the next. For longer or more complex assessments, give feedback within one or two weeks. Leverage your resources by enlisting others to help— invite other teachers and lawyers to provide feedback as well as asking your students to read and comment upon each other's work or their own work, comparing assessments with samples, checklists, or rubrics that you provide. Giving feedback is crucial to our students' success in law school and in practice. Start small, use a variety of feedback methods, and continue to reflect on what works, as suggested in Chapter 11.

Using Classroom Assessment Techniques to Improve Your Teaching

Classroom assessments help you see what students **are actually learning** during the class, allowing you to revise your teaching based on what you learn. One of our favorites is the **Minute Paper**. At any point in a class session, identify a discreet question or prompt to which you want students to respond. Put the question/ prompt on the board, slide, or a quarter sheet of paper. Ask students to take a minute to respond. Here are a few examples of the kinds of questions that can work well:

- "Identify a major factor in determining the 'best interests of the child.'"
- "What was the muddiest point of today's discussion?"
- "How confident are you about your ability to learn environmental law?"

Collect and scan through responses. Note general themes and give feedback in the next class, "Almost everyone had a question about federal preemption. Let me try to clarify ..."

Evaluating Students to Assign Grades— The Hardest Part of Assessment

For grades to have integrity, graded assessments must be valid and reliable. Students should only earn a grade after having multiple and varied assessments which are fairly administered (see Illustration 9-5).

Illustration 9-5. Evaluating Students to Assign Grades— Essential Elements

1. Use multiple assessments

2. Use a variety of assessments

3. Evaluate fairly:

   - Test what you teach—provide students with grading criteria in advance

   - Give students time to practice meeting criteria before they are graded

   - Use explicit criteria to ensure consistent grading

   - Show students how they met grading criteria—make the grading process also a learning process

Essential Elements

Use Multiple Assessments

Any of the assessments from Illustration 9-2 can contribute to students' grades. Example:

- 15% for class contributions (professional engagement in and outside of class);

- 25% for a midterm exam (half essay and half multiple-choice questions); and
- 60% on the final exam (essay and multiple-choice questions).

Use a Variety of Assessments

Because the practice of law is multi-dimensional and because students can demonstrate competency in many ways, use a range of graded assessments. See Illustration 9-2 for ideas.

Evaluate Fairly

Test what you teach and provide students with grading criteria in advance. Identify what you want students to learn by the end of the course, and check that your class sessions work towards those goals. As you construct your assessment instruments, review the goals to ensure that you test students on those goals. Provide students with a list of criteria or a rubric, such as the rubric in Illustration 9-3, to help them focus on those criteria and develop independent learning skills. If you are using oral presentations as an evaluative assessment, you could similarly describe the grading criteria and relative weights:

- Content—clear, organized and coherent—50%
- Visual aids—handouts, slides, props used to enhance content—20%
- Delivery—audible, clear, varied, responsive and within time limits—10%
- Creativity—shows innovation in presenting and engaging classmates—20%

By articulating the criteria in writing, we name what we mean by "analyze the following problem." Usually, we learn that we are expecting far more from students than we realized. Naming the criteria also keeps students from wasting energy trying to figure out what we want.

Give students time to practice meeting criteria before they are graded. It's only fair to allow students to practice and get feedback on exams, quizzes, drafts, or mock performances before they have to take assessments for a grade.

Use explicit criteria to ensure consistent grading. When teachers have explicit criteria, such as checklists or rubrics, they grade consistently and reliably, and maintain high expectations. They are also more efficient in the long term. Creating a rubric takes time but the early investment pays off during the actual grading.

Show students how they met grading criteria — make the grading process a learning process. If the graded assessment occurs before the end of the semester, hold a review session to go over the assessment or spend time in class reviewing it. Allow students to see or have the checklists or rubrics you used to assign their grades. Ask several students who have done well for permission to use their work as examples. Let students learn what good work can look like. If you want to reuse part of an assessment, allow students to review their exams and feedback material over a few weeks, taking notes, but not making copies.

If students want to meet with you to go over a grade, do the following.

- *Use the 24-hour rule.* Talk to students after they have had their graded assessment for 24 hours; this practice gives everyone a little breathing space.
- *Ask to meet with the student in person.* Meeting in person ensures a more productive conversation. We find email usually very ineffective.
- *Require students to review all materials and prepare questions before meeting with you individually.* This requirement makes the experience much more manageable and specific. If students challenge the grade, ask them to show you where they met the criteria in their assessment.
- *Almost never change a grade; if you do, only do it slowly and very carefully.* Follow your institution's rules about grade changes. If you learn of a mathematical error, review that exam and score sheet and cause of the mistake. If the error is in more than one place, consider how you can fix the problem across the class.

- *Limit the time in which students can talk to you about a graded assessment.* Once grades are out, give students two to four weeks to contact you with questions.

The Grading Process Itself— Designing and Using Rubrics/Scoring Sheets—One Way

As used below, the term "exam" means any graded assessment.

- Jump right in. Delaying the process makes it harder and more stressful.
- Figure out how much time you have until you must submit grades to the registrar.
- Skim seven to ten exams, developing checklists about effective responses.
- Draft the rubric, setting the weights of different components—is spotting tricky issues more important than spotting basic issues?
- Use the draft rubric to score ten exams. Set aside these first ten exams; track their numbers.
- Keeping a list, spreadsheet, or other method to track exam numbers, continue using rubrics to score exams. Revise the rubric as necessary—students always surprise us. (Have a "bonus" category for material that otherwise demonstrates attainment of course goals.)
- If the exam has more than one part, such as three essays, grade all students' Essay #1s only. When you have scored all Essay #1s, grade the Essay #2s. This approach helps reduce "drift," where performance on one part of an exam influences another part of that exam.
- Vary the order in which you grade. If you graded the first essays starting with low numbers, grade the second essays starting with the middle or highest numbers.

- Use a pencil or have white-out handy.
- Take breaks every hour, even if you don't think you need it. You'll be more efficient in the long run.
- When you have finished grading, revisit the first ten you graded. If you notice significant discrepancies from later ones, revise and continue to review until you find that the scores you gave earlier are consistent. Remember, a detailed scoring sheet will make you far more consistent.
- Total scores. You may want to review the handful of highest and lowest scores.
- Look for trends in scores. Capture that information with your course notes (see Chapter 11) for the next time you teach the course.
- Submit grades.
- Once you have submitted your grades, identify a few students who earned high scores on different parts of the exam. Request their permission for you to use their unidentified answers as samples of high quality student work.
- Take notes for yourself about grading to help you the next time.

Checklist for Assessing Student Learning

Illustration 9-6 is a checklist you can use as you work through the assessment process.

Illustration 9-6. Assessing Student Learning Checklist

Using assessment to improve student learning and your teaching

❏ **Identify discreet learning objectives**—the knowledge, skills and values you want students learn in your course.

❏ **Prepare and give assessment instruments**
  ❏ Identify the reason you are giving the assessment
  ❏ Be explicit about what you want students to do
  ❏ What is the assessment's content?
  ❏ How will you provide feedback?

❏ **Give feedback to students**
  ❏ **Specific.** Students get information about specific criteria.
  ❏ **Positive.** Students find out what they are doing well.
  ❏ **Corrective.** Students learn about their weaknesses and strategies to improve them.
  ❏ **Prompt.** Students get feedback while the assessment is fresh.

Evaluating students to assign grades

❏ Use multiple assessments
❏ Use a variety of assessments
❏ **Evaluate fairly:**
  ❏ Test what you teach—provide students with grading criteria in advance
  ❏ Give students time to practice meeting criteria before they are graded
  ❏ Use explicit criteria to ensure consistent grading
  ❏ Show students how they met grading criteria—make the grading process also a learning process

Engage in ongoing assessment

You will find examples of the concepts from this chapter in Appendix 9 on the book's website—http://lawteaching.org/resources.

Appendix 9-1: Assessment Instruments
  Peer Feedback Formative Assessment Exercise
  Midterm/Peer Feedback, Reflection Assessment
  Guidelines for Phase III: Reflection

International Environmental Law Quiz
Civil Procedure—Reflections on Civil Litigation

Appendix 9-2: Rubrics
   Torts Rubric
   Remedies Peer Review Rubric
   Client Letter Rubric
   Clinical Rubric-Performance Competencies
      Professionalism Rubric
      Reflective Paper/Journal Rubric

Chapter 10

Troubleshooting

The design of this chapter is quite different from the other chapters in this book because our goals are different. Our goals are to identify seven teaching challenges commonly experienced by adjunct law teachers and to offer our ideas for addressing those challenges. Consequently, each of this chapter's subsections describes a challenge and then suggests ways to address it. We have created this list of challenges based on comments teachers made at teaching workshops we have conducted and at law teaching conferences at which we have presented (collectively we have conducted more than 400 such workshops and presentations), from questions raised by law teachers with whom we have privately consulted, and from outstanding law teachers that we have studied. We also hope that the principles we discuss will allow you to address some of the challenges not addressed here. The chapter concludes with the common themes we identified in thinking through the challenges and writing the chapter.

Challenge 1: Unprepared or Unmotivated Students

The Challenge

This discussion addresses two, closely-related issues and a third more general issue. The first issue focuses on how we choose to react when one of our students is unprepared. The second issue focuses on that rare occasion when many students are unprepared. The third issue addresses what law teachers can do if their students seem generally under-motivated.

Addressing the Challenge

We start with two key takeaways from *What the Best Law Teachers Do*. Those two takeaways offer important preventive measures that law teachers can do to minimize student unpreparedness and disengagement. Students we interviewed repeatedly told us, "I would never be unprepared for _____'s class because she prepared for class so hard and cared so much about my learning." In other words, our effort and engagement often correlates with our students' effort and engagement. Second, when we interviewed the subjects for the study, we discovered that they all devote considerable time and effort to thinking through how they will motivate their students to learn. For example, one professional responsibility teacher would start each class by reading from the disciplinary roles from her state, often finding violations of the concepts the class was learning that day. Two of our subjects interviewed the lawyers who handled the cases they taught; the students reported feeling on the edge of their seats waiting for the lawyers' unique insights their teachers had tracked down for them.

We regard the single, unprepared student as the easiest issue. On the one hand, we feel strongly that publically embarrassing or berating the student is a significant mistake; teachers who do so often lose not only the unprepared student but many others as well. On the other hand, simply ignoring an unprepared student communicates that we do not care about preparation, which may create a risk that more students will be unprepared. Our preference is to let students know, in our syllabi and on the first day of class, that we expect students to diligently prepare for class but do not believe in publically embarrassing unprepared students; instead we will privately contact them and address the issue. We consistently follow through by contacting unprepared students. We have found that the most effective way to do so is to send an email that says something like, "I noticed you were not fully prepared for class today. I have no doubt you are capable of more. What can I do to better inspire you to prepare for my class?"

We suspect that widespread unpreparedness is rare. Unless you know for certain, it is probably better to assume that the students you happened to call on that day happened to be the unprepared students than to assume no students or only few students were prepared. Moreover, even if the unpreparedness is widespread, the reasons for the unpreparedness likely vary. Consequently, we suggest you start by sending emails along the lines suggested in the prior paragraph. If we really believed we had a persistent problem of student unpreparedness, we would address it by getting feedback and suggestions from the students. We may invite students to provide anonymous feedback in writing and then devote five or ten minutes of class to an open discussion.

If your students do seem generally under-motivated and unprepared, it is worth finding new ways to motivate the students. Ask them for input into the teaching methods that motivate them. Find relevant current events. Have students do personally-guided field trips in which they find examples of key concepts in the course as they play out in the real world.

Challenge 2: Disrespectful Students

The Challenge

This challenge can involve students being disrespectful to the law teacher, a faculty assistant, teaching assistant, or classmates. The literature and our colleagues' experiences suggest that faculty members and students of color and women are more frequently subjected to disrespectful student behavior than are white male teachers and students.

Addressing the Challenge

We have one syllabus-based suggestion for addressing this challenge and one general teaching suggestion, both of which we hope will minimize disrespect. However, because you may nevertheless encounter disrespectful students, we also offer a suggested process for addressing the issue and a final suggestion for addressing persistently problematic students.

We recommend setting expectations for respectful discourse in your syllabus. This approach may be most effective if you allow students to set the expectations for their interactions with you and each other (they nearly always include respectfulness, and, if they don't, you can ask them about their expectations in terms of respectful interactions). Those law teachers who set the expectations themselves can and should communicate in the syllabus an expectation that students respond respectfully to the teacher and each other.

Our general teaching suggestion is that you do everything you can to model the behaviors you expect of your students. Be extraordinarily well prepared. Be respectful of the students who disagree with you. Be positive and kind. Assume the best of your students. Admit errors. Think of yourself as modeling the behaviors you desire from your students.

Our suggested process to address disrespect in the classroom involves multiple steps:

1. Pause. Let the words hang there in silence; catch your own breath so you can manage the situation calmly and authentically.

2. Move the discussion outside of the class while also communicating that you are holding the students accountable. Ask the student to stay after class, i.e., "[insert student's name], can you please stay after class? I'd like to discuss your last comment with you privately."

3. Assume good faith. When you do speak with the student one-on-one, even if you believe that the student's manifestation of disrespect is the product of explicit or implicit bias, start with an assumption of good faith. Because the ultimate goal of any response to disrespectful behavior is to change that behavior in the future, a response that labels the student's behavior in a way that causes the student to be defensive (e.g., "that was a sexist thing to say") decreases the likelihood the student will change the behavior.

4. Don't assume it is personal. Bad student behavior is nearly always about the student and not the teacher.

5. Describe the behavior, your reaction to it, and why you reacted that way: "When you said or did [insert specific description], I [or the other student whom you observed being disrespected] felt [describe your response, e.g., angry, frustrated] because [explain why you felt that way, e.g., because your statement assumed…, because you spoke before (insert disrespected student's name) had finished her thought, because you interrupted (insert disrespected student's name)]."

6. Reference the class policy. As you may recall, my syllabus says, "[quote the relevant portion of your syllabus.]"

7. Make a specific demand: In the future, when you feel like [saying or doing] [insert what the student said or did], I want you to [insert specific desired new behavior.]

If all these suggestions fail with a persistently disrespectful student, get help. Have a trusted colleague sit in on your class and give you an insight into what is going on.

Challenge 3: Getting Lackluster or Poor Student Evaluations

The Challenge

Over the years, many law teachers have approached us for help when they believed they taught a class well yet received poor or lackluster student evaluations. It is worth noting that women and minorities consistently receive lower student evaluation scores, and recent studies suggest that students' impressions of teachers in the first three minutes seldom change by the end of the semester or year. On the other hand, many studies find that student evaluations of teaching are consistent with peer evaluations of teaching. We also know that law schools often rely heavily on student evaluations in evaluating adjunct faculty members, and we know that many adjuncts experience poor student evaluations as upsetting or embarrassing.

Addressing the Challenge

Please see Chapter 11 for a general discussion of addressing student evaluations.

All of the practices, attitudes, and relational behaviors described as being characteristic of good teachers (see Chapter 1) also positively influence student evaluations. We emphasize five such characteristics below.

First, manifesting respect for students and your confidence in their ability to learn can make a huge difference in students' initial and continuing impression of you. Students who perceive that you care to know them as individuals (both their names and their interests) are more likely to interpret the things you do as reflecting your efforts to help them learn. Students who believe you do not respect them are likely to feel insulted and disrespected, even if you adopt a wide variety of teaching practices aimed to help them learn. One example from the people we studied for *What the Best Law Teachers Do* illustrates this point. Some of the teachers had class-by-class syllabi from which they never varied; others adjusted their assignments every week to reflect student progress. The students who had the teachers who never waivered from their planned syllabi told us that their teachers respected them so much that their teachers made sure they stuck to their syllabi so students could manage their time. The students whose teachers' syllabi varied said their teachers respected them and wanted them to succeed so much that they adapted their lesson planning to the students' needs. Both groups of students interpreted their teachers' conduct in light of their belief that their teachers wanted them to succeed.

Second, authenticity can make a big difference in students' perceptions. Some of the people we studied for *What the Best Law Teachers Do* have wonderful senses of humor; others never crack a joke in class. What the students identified and focused on was their teachers' sincerity. They described their teachers as authentic, sincere, "very real," etc. In contrast, teachers who try to teach the way they were taught, even teachers who try to imitate their own favorite teachers, invariably struggle to win over their students.

Third, law teachers' preparation for class, on the first day of class and throughout the semester, makes a huge difference in student perceptions. When students believe their teachers have worked very hard to prepare for class, they are more likely to forgive errors, work hard, value their learning, and invest themselves in unfamiliar learning activities.

Fourth, teachers' passion for their subjects and for student success can influence student evaluations. One of us once listened as our daughter's geometry teacher explained, during the first three minutes of her back-to-school presentation, why she loves triangles. Her excitement about triangles convinced the parents in the room that she must be a good geometry teacher—anyone that excited about triangles could inspire any child to learn geometry. Teacher excitement conveys the message that something in the class is worth being excited about.

Fifth, it is important to avoid making the particular kinds of mistakes that most frustrate students. Return all exams, papers, and assignments promptly. Assign students an amount of class preparation that is reasonable for them and reasonable for you to cover in the following class session. Show up on time for class, start class and end class on time, and do everything you can to avoid cancelling a class session. (If you must cancel a class session or miss a grading deadline, be transparent about the causes and apologetic about your failure.) Never yell at students, embarrass them in class, or speak to them in a condescending tone.

Challenge 4: Doing Multiple Assessments without Killing Yourself

The Challenge

You've read Chapter 9, Assessing Student Learning, and believe that you need to administer multiple formative and summative assessments to improve student learning. You understand that practice and feedback helps students determine how to improve, and using multiple assessments allows you to assess a wider array of skills and knowledge and improve the accuracy of your conclusions about the students' success in learning the course material. The real challenge is implementation. You have a full-time practice! Providing feedback, even without assigning grades, can take hours of work, and, and the workload is exacerbated if the teacher is also grading the students' performance. In a large class, the burden seems insurmountable.

Addressing the Challenge

We have divided this discussion into two segments: (1) ideas for reasonably providing formative feedback in a large class, and (2) ideas for reasonably providing summative feedback in a large class. Keep in mind, however, that pre-final summative feedback also serves as formative feedback.

The following is a list of ideas for providing formative feedback that imposes manageable burden on the law teacher:

- Administer an essay question and then provide the students with a model answer to compare their answers.
- Administer an essay question and then provide the students with a rubric they can use to self-evaluate the work (the teacher can confirm that each student has used the rubric to evaluate the essay).
- Administer an essay question and then provide the students with a rubric they can use to peer-evaluate a colleague's work (the teacher can confirm that each student has used the rubric to evaluate the essay).
- Administer an essay question and then review a sample student answer.
- Administer an essay question and then lead a class discussion of how the students should have answered the question.
- Provide practice multiple-choice questions with answers and explanations.

The list of manageable burden summative assessments is equally lengthy:

- Administer one or more short multiple-choice tests.
- Administer short (one paragraph) essay questions (be sure to limit the length of your students' responses).
- Have students answer an essay question as a group (assuming groups of six students and 100 students, the teacher would only need to review less than 20 exams).
- Have students draft one or two contract clauses, will provisions, discovery requests, affirmative defenses, etc.
- Administer a short answer exam.
- Have students find real world examples (newspaper stories, etc.) of the legal concepts they are learning and write up an analysis of those stories.

Challenge 5: Addressing Controversial Topics in Class

The Challenge

We subscribe to the view that most law school courses raise issues that can be controversial. Employment Discrimination is an obvious example of a subject that can and does give rise to disagreement, but courses in labor law, civil liberties, tax, disability law, and most other subjects can raise thorny issues of race, class, gender, politics, and privilege. These issues create several, related challenges: How do we encourage free discussion and give all views a chance to be aired while keeping the focus on our core learning goals? How do we protect students from personal attacks or comments that are gratuitously disrespectful? How do we manage our own reactions to upsetting student remarks?

Addressing the Challenge

As a foundational matter, we believe that ignoring or suppressing discussion of controversial issues is probably the worst choice. If you allow free discussion of even one policy issue, your failure to permit discussion of an issue about race or gender or politics, because you are concerned students will be upset, has the potential to send a message that you regard the issues you are ignoring as unimportant. Rather than ignoring such topics, acknowledge your worries about the potential for discord, ask the students to be sensitive to each other, and then open up the subjects. The remainder of this discussion focuses on our suggestions for managing the discussion effectively.

If you believe there are any topics about which students may become agitated, it is important that the class agree to expectations for respectful communication. Ideally, involve your students in (1) setting those expectations and (2) discussing the value of different perspectives to the learning process. You may also want your students to engage in an exercise in which each of them imagines another student saying something with which the student disagrees and planning how she or he will listen and respond respectfully.

If you wish to set the expectations yourself, your expectations might include: (1) listening respectfully (and repeating the key point of the person who just spoke) before speaking; (2) assuming good intentions of others and avoiding personal attacks or global statements about affinity groups; (3) speaking only to add new points rather than to repeat previously made arguments or communicate agreement with a previous speaker; and (4) thinking through how your words might be heard before speaking—even if that means that you volunteer to speak and then wait 10–15 seconds before speaking. If you decide to include an expectation that students should only speak to add new points, give your students an opportunity to communicate agreement in some other way, such as by applauding or waving a hand.

You also may need to set other types of expectations. For example, consider imposing a time limit on the duration of the discussion or on how long each student may speak. Likewise, your students need to know that you are managing the discussion and using the discussion to further course goals. Some teachers find it helpful to give students space to be upset, allowing students to decide to leave the room for a moment to collect their emotions.

Our next set of suggestions are ideas about what you can do during the heated discussion. In facing challenging issues, we first need to be aware of our own responses. In these situations, students especially need to see us model calm and constructive leadership. Think of yourself as someone responding to a health emergency or 911 call. The first rule is to stay calm. Take a deep breath. Try to disengage for a minute and consider the view of the classroom dynamic from above the class. What just happened? Why might a student have reacted that way? We can name the challenge, use silence, and ask students to pause and reflect on what just happened in the classroom. "I see that many of you are uncomfortable with the opinion just stated, that health insurance should never cover the cost of an abortion. Before we continue, let's pause for a minute to think about why some of us might hold that view." We want students' to learn how to listen to controversial views and to try to understand others' perspectives.

As noted above, it is critical that you make sure you retain control of the discussion; students responding to students is often a sign of a good discussion—unless the emotions have gotten out of hand. Some teachers find it helpful to give students time to write about an issue, either before launching into the issue or if the discussion gets heated. It is helpful, before letting students evaluate or respond to the arguments on a topic, to have the students identify all the possible arguments and what a supporter of each argument might say to defend his or her argument. Likewise, having students volunteer to defend an argument with which they disagree can be a powerful learning tool for future lawyers.

You may be concerned that addressing controversial issues will take up valuable class time that could be otherwise used to help students learn. We suggest that understanding others' perspectives and learning how to address controversy with respect and dignity is an important learning objective in any class. If you have created a positive classroom environment, anticipated issues in advance, and seek to have students learn from these discussions, you will have done your students a service.

If a student does become particularly upset, we make it a point to contact the student after class, ask the student how he or she is doing, invite the student to talk to us about concerns or just share her or his reaction, and otherwise provide input.

Our final thoughts return to the idea of doing your best to manage your own emotional reactions to a discussion. It is always a mistake to yell at or otherwise berate a student based on a comment the student made in class. You can and should, of course, enforce agreed-upon expectations, such as listening respectfully and avoiding personal attacks or global assumptions about affinity groups. We suggest you be transparent as you can (e.g., "I am finding myself feeling agitated, but I want to make sure everyone in this room feels respected and feels safe to make arguments with which I disagree, so I am … [explain what you are doing to manage your feelings and encourage discussion, such as waiting 20 seconds to collect your thoughts and starting by summarizing the key points you just heard].")

Thinking exercise: Think back to the best discussion of a difficult subject you have participated in as a teacher or a student. What made the discussion so effective? What did the teacher do?

Challenge 6: Being Asked a Question That You Are Unable to Answer in the Moment or Making a Mistake in Class

The Challenge

At the outset, it is worth noting that being unable to conclusively respond to a student's question or making a mistake in class is not limited to new or inexperienced law teachers; we believe that, if we are doing our jobs well, we all have both types of moments throughout our careers. While we believe that preparation and experience minimize both types of challenges, we also regard a complex, perceptive student question for which there is no easy answer as a success. We believe not only that mistakes are inevitable but, in fact, are more likely if we are taking the healthy teaching risks essential to growth as a law teacher.

Addressing the Challenge

The very best thing we can do to respond to most questions for which we do not have a ready answer is to copy the approach used by teachers we studied for *What the Best Law Teachers Do*. The teachers we studied typically (1) acknowledged that they do not have a ready answer to the student's question; (2) showed delight that a student asked a question for which they do not have a ready answer; (3) offered a tentative answer, making it clear not only that their answer was tentative, but also speaking aloud their process in generating their answer (modeling how a lawyer thinks through knotty questions); (4) promised to get back to the class with a more definitive response; and (5) did get back to their students in the next class with a more definitive response, identifying and congratulating the student who asked the question.

Mistakes are even easier to address. We find it easiest to just admit the mistake, correct the error, and move on as if nothing significant has occurred.

The approaches we recommend have two common features. As we have suggested throughout this chapter and throughout the book, authenticity works. If we are transparent about the limits of our knowledge, students feel more connected to us and perceive us to be so confident about our expertise that we are comfortable acknowledging our limitations. Moreover, if students perceive that we work hard to help them learn, and we put a lot of care and commitment into our teaching, they readily forgive our errors and failings, especially if we take responsibility for them rather than hiding or obscuring them. Likewise, respect for students works. When students feel we respect them enough to celebrate their insightful questions, find answers to those questions, and acknowledge our errors, they invest themselves more in our classes and feel better about their learning experiences.

Challenge 7: Students Do Not Read: (1) The Instructions on Exams, (2) Assignment Instructions, (3) Emails, or (4) the Syllabus

The Challenge

We very commonly hear complaints about students failing to read things their teachers wanted them to have read. Generally, the missed information relates to deadlines and formatting and results in students making excuses for submitting late assignments or work products that fail to comply with stated expectations.

Addressing the Challenge

We think it is helpful to consider our exam and assignment instructions, our emails and our syllabi as containing information we want our students to learn. This conceptual approach suggests a few simple practices would help. First, repeat the things you want your students to remember. Repetition was a common teaching practices among the teachers we studied for *What the Best Law Teachers Do*. Repetition can help students internalize deadlines and instructions. This information should be available to students in writing in the syllabus, in a handout, or both. And we can remind students of this information orally or in writing on the board or on a slide. Second, if students understand they will be held accountable for deadlines, and you follow through and do hold them accountable, they will quickly adapt. Third, adult learners tend to respond to expectations they regard as meaningful. As a practitioner, you can explain to students that meeting deadlines and complying with instructions are fundamental aspects of professionalism. To the extent you can create formatting rules consistent with your local court rules and direct your students to find your rules in the local court rules, you can accomplish your goals while also getting your students to see the importance of local rules.

Conclusion: Common Themes

As our responses to all of the challenges addressed in this chapter reflect, addressing most of the challenges law teachers face involves applying the principles discussed throughout this book. Core principles of good teaching, including respect for students, caring about their learning, preparation, creativity, focus on learning goals, authenticity, and integrity are generally relevant to producing learning and specifically relevant to addressing the challenges commonly faced by law teachers.

Chapter 11

Developing as a Teacher

The central aim of this book is to produce significant student learning by designing, delivering, and assessing law school courses and classes. An underlying premise is that teachers play a meaningful role in students' learning. The focus of this chapter is on your continued professional development as teachers. How can we enhance our students' learning by continuing to improve our teaching?

Sustaining a Teaching Practice

Nearly all adjunct professors are motivated primarily by the intrinsic rewards of teaching. This intrinsic motivation spurs adjuncts to seek feedback on their performance and new strategies to improve their teaching.

Although continued professional development as teachers can provide great satisfaction and reward, we should acknowledge the obstacles that hinder growth. Faculty misconceptions about teaching and learning present obstacles. Misconceptions include (1) if you know the content well, you can teach well; (2) you should master one teaching technique that suits your style and stick with it; and (3) good teachers are born, not made. Research debunks all of these myths: (1) effective teaching requires knowledge of content coupled with pedagogical skill; (2) no single teaching method works for every student or accomplishes every educational goal; and (3) successful teachers learn how to teach and continue to improve their skills throughout their careers. Further, continuing to develop teaching skills, a complex, human activity, is not easy. As we learn more about teaching and learning, we may uncover shortcomings in our current philosophy and practice. It is common for us to struggle as we try new methods. Sustained development in teaching requires hard work and perseverance.

The challenges and rewards of ongoing efforts to improve teaching apply to all faculty, not just new teachers or those who are struggling in the classroom. All of us can enhance our effectiveness through reflection, feedback, and innovation.

Most models of teaching development involve several stages: instructional awareness, formative feedback, pedagogical knowledge, implementation, and assessment.

- **Instructional awareness.** The first step in the process of improving instruction is to increase our understanding of our own teaching philosophy and practices. What do we believe are the purposes of legal education and our roles as teachers? What assumptions do we make about teaching and learning? What behaviors do we exhibit when we interact with students in and out of the classroom? Are our teaching methods consistent with our educational philosophy?
- **Formative feedback.** Formative feedback is critical to improving teaching and learning. To make effective changes in teaching, we need to know the strengths and weaknesses of our current practices and their effect on students' learning. We can gather that information from ourselves, students, colleagues, and consultants.
- **Pedagogical knowledge.** Deeper understanding of student learning and teaching methods can help us put the feedback we receive in context. We can gain valuable insights from scholarship about learning theory and student motivation. Likewise, the literature on teaching methods, instructional design, educational technology, and assessment inform our choices about appropriate adjustments in our teaching.
- **Implementation.** Teaching improvement occurs through changes in our teaching philosophy, attitudes, and behavior. Numerous resources are available to assist us at this stage— books, articles, websites, and videos on teaching; discussions with colleagues; working with consultants. To be effective,

these changes should be incremental and systematic. A good start in teaching improvement could entail one or two small changes implemented throughout a course.

- **Assessment**. The final stage is for us to evaluate the effectiveness of our teaching improvement efforts. Did our changes in philosophy, attitudes, and practices improve our teaching and our students' learning? This information forms the basis for the next cycle in our teaching development.

Many types of faculty development activities are available for teachers who want to increase their effectiveness. We surveyed law teachers throughout the United States regarding their participation in activities to improve teaching. These teaching improvement activities are discussed below. Many of these take some time but are very low cost.

Self-Assessment, Reflection, and Study

Many faculty members provide their own faculty development through individual assessment, reflection, and study. For many of us, the most important source of information is our own observations and reflection on our teaching.

Benefits of Reflective Practice

Self-study and reflection can help us to become more aware of our teaching assumptions and behaviors, to articulate a coherent teaching rationale, and to make informed changes in our instructional practices. Most teachers have deeply ingrained assumptions about teaching and learning, which affect teaching behavior. To grow as teachers, we must identify our current assumptions and behavior that may be hindering our effectiveness. Our observations and reflection can reveal patterns of behavior, habitual responses, underlying motivations, and aspects of our teaching that need improvement. Reflective teachers are able to explain the rationale behind their teaching. That rationale can give us confidence and serve as the foundation for our teaching choices. As a result of examining assumptions and developing a rationale, reflective teachers modify their plans, attitudes, and actions in the classroom.

These benefits of reflective practice are supported by empirical research. Our survey respondents concluded that reflection on their teaching before and after class is effective in increasing their awareness of their teaching philosophy and practices, improving their level of confidence, and increasing their enthusiasm and passion for teaching. Further, law teachers rated reflection (thinking about teaching and keeping a journal about teaching) as the faculty development activities most effective in producing changes in their teaching practices.

Self-Assessment

Evaluation forms and inventories can help teachers engage in self-assessment. We can analyze our teaching behaviors by completing the same course evaluation form that the students fill out at the end of the term. The results can be revealing. Most teachers' self-assessments of their strengths and weaknesses agree with their students' assessments.

Inventories help teachers assess the presence, absence, and extent of instructional behaviors. Inventories adapted to legal education allow us assess our teaching in the context of seven empirically derived principles for enhancing learning: Encouraging student-faculty contact; fostering cooperation among students; encouraging active learning, giving prompt feedback; emphasizing time on task; communicating high expectations; and respecting diverse talents and ways of learning. All seven inventories are accessible on the book's website.

Teaching Journal

An excellent tool for reflection is a teaching journal. The process of keeping a professional journal promotes reflection. Journals are a useful device for creating a comprehensive account of our experience. The journal is a place to record problems, successes, strategies for improvement, and ideas for subsequent classes. Because journal entries are made close in time to our experiences, they are often more accurate than our recollections months after the events. Journal writing helps us to clarify our assumptions and theories about teaching and learning, to evaluate the effectiveness of instructional practices, and to identify alternative methods to try in the future. Further, teaching journals are tools for setting goals, planning individual class sessions, and restructuring courses. We can use journals to analyze problems and to work through the strong emotions that accompany teaching. Finally, journal writing can be a vehicle for us to integrate our personal and professional selves and to engage in a lifelong, reflective learning process.

Law teachers who keep a teaching journal rated it as the single most effective faculty development device for prompting actual changes in teaching behavior. Yet, only 9% of the respondents to our survey keep a teaching journal. Why? Keeping a teaching journal is not easy. It takes time, energy, and discipline. And journal writing does not fit the learning style preference of every teacher; some of us are more comfortable talking about our experiences than writing about them.

Several practical aspects of the journal writing process can make it more fun and valuable:

- Space. Find a comfortable place to write free of distractions—in the office with the door closed, in a coffee shop, or at home in a comfortable chair.
- Time. Schedule time for journal writing; for example, twice a week for twenty minutes or after each class for ten minutes.
- Format. There are many options to fit individual preferences—bound journal books, three ring binders, an artist's sketchbook, a computer.
- Commitment. Put journal time on the calendar and treat it like a professional appointment.
- Trust the process. Don't censor. Insight and progress can follow paragraphs of bland, uninspired writing.
- Content. Free-writing in which we describe and explore our experiences is a common form of journaling. An alternative

is to write in response to a prompt. You can find reflection prompts on the book's website, Appendix 11.

Print and Electronic Resources

Numerous print and electronic resources facilitate self-directed faculty development. Journal articles, books, newsletters, videos, and websites address the theory and practice of teaching and learning. Law teachers regularly engage in this type of development—over 80% of our survey respondents reported reading journal articles on teaching and learning and 33% read books on those topics. Using these resources can help us improve our teaching in several ways—by causing us to reflect on our instructional practices, by giving us ideas, and by inspiring us to take reasonable risks and exert the effort needed to improve teaching and learning. The Selected Resources section at the end of this book provides a gateway to some of our other work on the teaching and learning.

Formative Feedback from Students

Feedback from students about our teaching and their learning is an important part of faculty development. Over 90% of our survey respondents review student evaluations after the course. In addition, about 50% of the respondents gather feedback from students about teaching effectiveness during the course.

Student Evaluations

Extensive empirical research in higher education demonstrates the value of student evaluations for faculty development. Dozens of studies reveal a persistent positive effect of written feedback from students on subsequent teaching effectiveness. Written student comments provide us with formative feedback and helpful suggestions regarding our clarity, delivery, organization, punctuality, fairness, demeanor, and availability outside of class.

Despite the potential benefits of end-of-the-term student evaluations for faculty development, some law teachers are reluctant to use them for development purposes. Their reluctance may come from a lack of confidence in the value of student evaluations and the pain that comes from reviewing negative comments. The following ideas may help maximize the usefulness of student evaluations and minimize the discomfort from negative comments.

- Look at the numerical evaluations and read quickly though the comments to get an overall sense of the students' reaction to the course. The first time though the evaluations, many teachers focus on the lower scores and negative comments.
- Review the numerical evaluations a second time to analyze the results. Compare the scores on each item to scores from the previous time or two that you taught the course. Pay attention to the trend in the scores.
- Review the comments a second time to identify themes. Articulate in writing several categories of positive comments. Identify in writing one or two areas in which the students made negative comments or suggested improvement. Compare the positive and negative themes to comments in previous student evaluations.
- Choose an area or two to address the next time you teach the course. Make incremental, not wholesale, changes.
- Try to ignore isolated mean comments, such as "I learned nothing in this course" or "Professor X should be fired." These types of comments are a reflection on the commentator's problems, not our teaching.
- Have a colleague or consultant review your student evaluations. Another set of eyes can help us see the positive aspects of the evaluations and can assist us in identifying trends, themes, and appropriate adjustments to make in the future.

Feedback from Students during the Course

Gathering formative feedback from students during the course helps us improve our teaching. Our survey respondents rated "gathering and reviewing feedback from students about own teaching during a course" as an effective means of improving teaching in three ways: improving their level of confidence in their teaching, increasing their enthusiasm and passion for teaching, and making changes in teaching practices. The classroom assessment methods described in Chapter 9 help teachers gather feedback from students about their learning and make reasonable adjustments in teaching methods during the rest of the course to maximize students' learning.

Teachers can design short written questionnaires to obtain detailed feedback from students during the course to improve teaching. The questionnaire can focus on a specific aspect of teaching or the course as a whole. For example, the questionnaire could ask three questions: (1) What teaching/learning methods have been *most* effective for you in this course? (2) What teaching/learning methods have been *least* effective for you in this course? (3) What other teaching/learning methods should we try in this course?

Keep the questionnaire process simple. Design a one-page form with three to five questions. Explain to students the purpose of the questionnaire—to gather feedback to make your teaching and their learning more effective. Distribute the form in class. Have your students respond anonymously. Collect and review the responses, looking for prevalent themes. Within a week, report briefly to the class about the common responses to each of the questions. Inform students of at least one suggestion that you intend to implement.

Teachers who use questionnaires during the course can experience several types of benefits. First, students' responses should provide specific feedback and suggestions to improve teaching and learning. Further, the process of seeking feedback from students and implementing reasonable suggestions shows our deep respect for students. Many students will respond by working hard to achieve the goals of the course. Finally, the questionnaire process demonstrates a critical life-long, professional skill—welcoming and profiting from constructive feedback.

Collaborating with Colleagues

Our colleagues are valuable teaching development resources. Over 90% of our survey respondents talk with colleagues about teaching as one form of faculty development. Around 50% have observed a colleague's classes to provide feedback or had fellow teachers observe their classes for development purposes.

Discussions with Colleagues

Talking with colleagues about teaching and learning is a common and effective type of development activity. In our survey, law teachers rated this activity as effective on every dimension of teaching development:

- Increasing their awareness of their own teaching practice and philosophy;
- Increasing their knowledge of teaching and learning principles;
- Improving their level of confidence in their teaching;
- Increasing their enthusiasm or passion for teaching; and
- Making changes in their teaching practices.

Peer Observations and Feedback

Peer observations can be especially valuable if pairs of colleagues agree to observe one another's classes. The reciprocal nature of the observations creates mutual vulnerability and shared responsibility. The colleagues can follow a three-step process.

First, the colleagues meet for a pre-observation conference. They discuss their approaches to teaching, goals for the course as a whole and class to be observed, material for the class, expectations for student preparation, what students will do during the class, and the teaching methods to be used. Most importantly, they tell one another the specific types of feedback they would like to receive. Areas for feedback could include organization, clarity, use of visual aids, types of questions, handling student responses, teacher's verbal and nonverbal communication, level of student engagement during class, number of women and men speaking in class, etc.

Second, the pairs visit each other's classes and gather the requested feedback. For example, if the teacher requests feedback on questioning, the observer could write out every question the teacher asks during the class; if the teacher wants feedback on student engagement, the observer could note what the students are doing at one-minute intervals during the class.

Third, the colleagues meet for a post-observation conference. Those discussions should include the specific feedback requested in the pre-observation conference, both teachers' positive and negative reactions, the extent to which the goals for the class were accomplished, and an exploration of alternative methods to achieve course objectives.

In addition to classroom visits, colleagues are ideally situated to help one another with course design, materials, and evaluation instruments. Peers can provide formative feedback on syllabi, course web pages, readings and other assignments. Colleagues can be especially helpful in reviewing the materials related to evaluating student work: quizzes and tests (both graded and ungraded) as well as paper and presentation assignments.

Consultants

Teaching development consultants can be national "experts" from outside of the institution, members of a university teaching excellence center, or faculty members from within the law school with expertise in teaching and learning. The roles of consultants and colleagues in faculty development can overlap quite a bit. Consultants or colleagues can conduct classroom observations, review course materials, engage in individual coaching, and work with peers who record their teaching.

Video recording can be a particularly powerful device for assessing and improving our classroom communication skills. A video of a class provides accurate, reliable, audio and visual feedback of several areas of our classroom performance:

- Verbal communication—clarity of speech, volume, verbal ticks
- Visual aids—legibility of board work, visual impact of computer presentations
- Nonverbal behavior—eye contact, movement, gestures
- Questioning—types of questions we ask and how we handle student responses
- Other presentation skills, including organization, flow, pacing, and variety in methods.

Despite the value of video recording in faculty development, many teachers are reluctant to be recorded. Only 17% of our survey respondents report viewing a video of their own teaching. Their reluctance may be due to anxiety about the recording and review, which can reveal communication glitches and dramatically illustrate to teachers the disparity between their self-image and the behavior they see on the video.

Several techniques can minimize the anxiety and maximize the value of video recording and review.

1. Select a "typical" class to be recorded. Explain to students that the purpose of the video is to provide feedback on your teaching, not to record their performance.
2. View the video soon after the class while the class is fresh in your mind. View the recording once to get used to seeing yourself on video and to get over the natural tendency to focus on minor distractions—Do I really sound like that? Look like that? Have those mannerisms?
3. View the video a second time with a supportive colleague who can provide perspective and can help you focus on specific strengths and weaknesses rather than the minor distractions (voice, appearance) that have little to do with effective teaching.
4. Use a checklist to help you assess significant components of teaching, such as organization, visual aids, clarity of presentation, questioning, and student participation.
5. Use the video to generate detailed data on specific aspects of your teaching. For example, record every question you ask and analyze the clarity and depth of each question. Or

keep track of what is happening at minute intervals—
teacher talk? Student question? Student comment? Exercise?

6. With the assistance of a colleague or consultant, choose one
    or two aspects of your teaching to address in response to the
    feedback from your review of the video.

7. Keep control of the video. It is yours. Save it to review in
    the future and compare to subsequent videos of your teach-
    ing. Or destroy it if that makes you more comfortable.

Teaching Workshops and Conferences

Teaching effectiveness workshops rank among the most popular
faculty development activities. Approximately half of law teachers
responding to our faculty development survey report attending a
workshop on pedagogy at their own institution. About one quarter
of the respondents attended a national or regional teaching conference, sponsored by Association of American Law Schools,
CALI, the Legal Writing Institute, the Society of American Law
Teachers, or the Institute for Law Teaching and Learning. Even
though your institution may not provide funds for you to travel to
a national conference, you may find local or regional conferences
that do not charge fees.

Among the twenty-two activities assessed in the faculty development survey, attending a national or regional conference or
workshop was among the most effective. Attending these conferences was rated as the most effective in three dimensions: (1) increasing a teacher's knowledge of teaching and learning principles;
(2) improving a teacher's confidence in teaching; and (3) increasing a teacher's enthusiasm and passion for teaching. The value of
attending national or regional conferences is further supported by
a survey that we conducted five years after an AALS teaching and
learning conference. Most of the respondents reported that their
attendance at the conference increased their reflection on teaching
methods (97%), knowledge of teaching and learning principles
(96%), awareness of their own teaching philosophy (95%), confidence (71%), and enthusiasm for teaching (70%). In addition,

93% of the respondents implemented changes in their teaching practices as a result of the conference.

Checklist for Teaching Development

Illustration 11-1 is a checklist you can use to guide your continued development as a teacher.

Illustration 11-1. Teaching Development Checklist

❏   **Self assessment, reflection, and study**
  ❏   Thinking about effective teaching methods before and after class
  ❏   Reading books and articles on teaching and learning
  ❏   Completing inventories on teaching practices
  ❏   Keeping a teaching journal

❏   **Formative feedback from students**
  ❏   Reviewing student evaluations of your teaching after the course
  ❏   Gathering feedback from students on your teaching during the course

❏   **Collaborating with colleagues**
  ❏   Talking with colleagues about teaching and learning
  ❏   Observing a colleague's class and providing feedback
  ❏   Having a colleague observe your class and provide feedback

❏   **Working with a consultant**
  ❏   Receiving individual coaching on teaching strengths and weaknesses
  ❏   Reviewing video of your teaching

❏   **Teaching workshops and conferences**
  ❏   Attending a national or regional conference on teaching and learning
  ❏   Attending a workshop at your institution on teaching and learning

You will find examples of the concepts from this chapter in Appendix 11 on the book's website—http://lawteaching.org/resources.

Appendix 11-1: Principles for Enhancing Student Learning—
            Faculty Inventory

Appendix 11-2: Reflection Prompts

Selected Resources —
Books, Articles, Newsletters, Videos, and Websites

The print and electronic literature on teaching and learning in higher education and law school is enormous. Excellent resources addressing both theory and practice abound for teachers who want to know more and to improve their skills. We encourage you to explore that literature. Rather than create pages and pages of resources, we have listed below only those works that one or more of the three of us authored or are otherwise involved in.

Books

Gerald F. Hess & Steven Friedland, Techniques for Teaching Law (1999).

Gerald F. Hess & Steven Friedland, Teaching the Law School Curriculum (2004).

Gerald F. Hess, Steven Friedland, Sophie M. Sparrow & Michael Hunter Schwartz, Techniques for Teaching Law II (2011).

Michael Hunter Schwartz, Expert Learning for Law Students (2d ed. 2008).

Michael Hunter Schwartz, Gerald F. Hess & Sophie M. Sparrow, What the Best Law Teachers Do (2014).

Sophie M. Sparrow, Gerald F. Hess & Michael Hunter Schwartz, Teaching Law By Design for Adjuncts (2010).

EILEEN SCALLEN, SOPHIE M. SPARROW, & CLIFF ZIMMERMAN, WORKING TOGETHER IN LAW: TEAMWORK AND SMALL GROUP SKILLS FOR LEGAL PROFESSIONALS (2014).

Articles and Book Chapters

Gerald F. Hess, *Qualitative Research on Legal Education: Studying Outstanding Law Teachers,* 51 ALBERTA L. REV. 925 (2014).

Gerald F. Hess, *Blended Courses in Law School: The Best of Online and Face-to-Face Learning?* 45 McGEORGE L. REV. 51 (2013).

Gerald F. Hess, *Value of Variety: An Organizing Principle to Enhance Teaching and Learning,* 3 ELON L. REV. 65 (2011).

Gerald F. Hess & Earl Martin, *Developing a Skills and Professionalism Curriculum—Process and Product,* 41 U. TOLEDO L. REV 327 (2010).

Gerald F. Hess & Steven Gerst, *Professional Skills and Values in Legal Education: The GPS Model,* 43 VALPARAISO U. L. REV. 513 (2009).

Gerald F. Hess, *Collaborative Course Design: Not My Course, Not Their Course, But Our Course,* 47 WASHBURN L. REV. 367 (2007).

Gerald F. Hess, *Heads and Hearts: The Teaching and Learning Environment in Law School,* 52 J. LEGAL EDUC. 75 (2002).

Gerald F. Hess, *Improving Teaching and Learning in Law School: Faculty Development Research, Principles, and Programs,* 12 WIDENER L. REV. 443 (2006).

Gerald F. Hess, *Learning to Think Like a Teacher: Reflective Journals for Legal Educators,* 38 GONZAGA L. REV. 129 (2003).

Gerald F. Hess, *Listening to Our Students: Obstructing and Enhancing Learning in Law School,* 31 U.S.F. L. REV. 941 (1997).

Gerald F. Hess, *Student Involvement in Improving Law Teaching and Learning,* 67 U.M.K.C. L. REV. 443 (2006).

Gerald F. Hess & Sophie M. Sparrow, *What Helps Law Professors Develop as Teachers?—An Empirical Study,* 14 WIDENER L. REV. 149 (2008).

Michael Hunter Schwartz, *Engaging First-Year Law Students by Treating Them Like Colleagues* (co-authored with Washburn Law Student Scott Abbott) in Brockmann/Pilniok (eds.), STUDIENEINGANGSPHASE IN DER RECHTSWISSENSCHAFT (2014).

Michael Hunter Schwartz, *Learning Theory and Teaching Theory* in BUILDING ON BEST PRACTICES (2015).

Michael Hunter Schwartz, *50 More Years of CLEO Scholars: The Past, the Present and a Vision for the Future*, 48 VALPARAISO L. REV. 1 (2014).

Michael Hunter Schwartz, *Improving Legal Education by Improving Casebooks: Fourteen Things Casebooks Can Do Differently to Move Legal Education Forward*, 3 ELON L. REV. 27 (2011).

Michael Hunter Schwartz, *Teaching Law Students to be Self-Regulated Learners*, 2003 MICH. STATE L. REV. 447 (2003).

Michael Hunter Schwartz, *Teaching Law by Design: How Learning Theory and Instructional Design Can Inform and Reform Law Teaching*, 38 SAN DIEGO L. REV. 347 (2001).

Michael Hunter Schwartz, *Washburn's Reform Process, Results and Analysis* in REFORMING LEGAL EDUCATION (co-authored with Jeremiah Ho) (2012).

Sophie Sparrow, *Team-Based Learning in Law*, 18 LEG. WRITING 53 (2013).

Sophie Sparrow, *Can They Work Well on a Team? Assessing Students' Collaborative Skills*, 38 WM. MITCHELL L. REV. 1162 (2012).

Sophie Sparrow, *Using Individual and Group Multiple-Choice Quizzes to Deepen Students' Learning*, 3 ELON L. REV. 1 (2011).

Sophie Sparrow, *Practicing Civility in the Legal Writing Course: Helping Law Students Learn Professionalism*, 13 J. LEG. WRITING 113 (2007).

Sophie Sparrow, *Describing the Ball: Improve Teaching by Using Rubrics—Explicit Grading* Criteria, 2004 MICH. ST. L. REV. 1.

Videos

Gerald F. Hess, Paula Lustbader, Laurie Zimet, PRINCIPLES TO ENHANCE LEGAL EDUCATION (Inst. for L. Sch. Teaching 2001).

Gerald F. Hess, Paula Lustbader, Laurie Zimet, TEACH TO THE WHOLE CLASS: BARRIERS AND PATHWAYS TO LEARNING (Inst. for L. Sch. Teaching 1997).

Michael Hunter Schwartz, Podcast and Supporting Materials, *Expert Learning for Law Students*, LSAC ACADEMIC ASSISTANCE WEBSITE (Spring 2009).

Institute for Law Teaching and Learning Website — http://lawteaching.org

The Institute for Law Teaching and Learning is sponsored by Gonzaga University School of Law, Washburn University School of Law, and the University of Arkansas at Little Rock, William H. Bowen School of Law. Resources available on this website include:

- *THE LAW TEACHER newsletter*
- *Article of the Month*
- *Idea of the Month*
- *Books and articles on teaching and learning—full text*
- *Videos on teaching and learning*
- *Assessment resources*
- *Team Based Learning resources*

About the Context and Practice Series

The principles recommended in *Teaching Law By Design for Adjuncts* (and in the larger book, *Teaching Law by Design*, Second Edition, 2016) are embodied in Carolina Academic Press's Context and Practice Casebook Series. Edited by Michael Hunter Schwartz in consultation with Gerry Hess, the Context and Practice texts are designed based on modern educational theory and provide law teachers with the materials they need to better prepare their students not just to think like lawyers, but to practice like them.

The books in these series offer many improvements to traditional law texts. Books in the Context and Practice Series provide authentic, law practice problems, materials (such as pleadings, contracts, and police reports) and instructional resources designed to contextualize students' doctrinal learning and help students build lawyering skills; include questions and problems that prompt readers to question, reflect, and analyze as they read; engage students in developing their professional identities; guide students' development of self-directed learning strategies; and include teachers' manuals that make it easy to use multiple methods of instruction, to implement meaningful assessment practices without killing oneself, and to emphasize active learning.

For more information on series, go to http://www.cap-press.com/p/CAP. For a listing of available and forthcoming titles, click on the flier link at the bottom of the page.

Index

active learning, 4–5, 7, 10, 40,
56, 68, 73–74, 77–78, 105,
118, 160
examples, 11, 20, 30, 37, 44,
47, 51, 64, 84, 86–87, 90,
92–101, 107–109, 111,
115, 118–120, 122, 125,
131–132, 135, 138, 143,
149, 170
exercises, 9–10, 16, 18, 47,
55, 64, 68–69, 71, 73–74,
90–92, 94, 96, 102–104,
107
experiential, 64, 73, 91–
109
large group, 44, 75, 118,
120–122
minute papers, 118
presentations, 80, 94, 99,
101, 108, 117, 126,
128, 134, 141, 167
problem-solving, 36
role-plays, 108, 126
simulations, 5, 10, 16,
43–44, 73, 76, 91, 94,
100, 108, 126, 128

small group, 6, 11, 18, 31,
44, 73, 75–76, 78, 85,
101–102, 118–119, 122
think-write-pair-share, 73
writing, 4, 10–11, 19–20,
25, 32, 34, 44, 47–49,
68, 73–74, 80, 86, 88,
91, 94, 105, 112, 118–
119, 134, 141, 143,
154, 161, 163, 168
value of, 108, 150, 162–163,
167–168
adult learning theory, 6
affect, 8, 40, 59, 95, 98, 104,
116, 159
ambiguity, 86–87, 111, 127
arguments, 19, 59–60, 70, 76,
100–101, 104, 115, 118, 120,
122, 126, 150–152
assessment, 5, 12, 25, 28–29,
35–36, 45–46, 64, 102, 105,
125–130, 132–138, 147–148,
158–160, 164, 169
characteristics, 11, 27, 41,
60, 121, 146
checklist, 23, 36, 50, 64, 83,
89, 108, 123–124, 129,
132, 135–138, 167, 169

criteria, 11, 57, 129–130, 133–135, 138
cycle, 56, 159
fair, 28, 134
formative, 7, 11–12, 46, 113, 121–124, 138, 147–148, 158, 162–163, 166, 169
grading, 33–35, 133–138, 147–148
instruments, 28, 125–126, 134, 138, 166
learning objectives, 35, 65, 72, 77, 80, 85–86, 89, 108, 113–117, 124–125, 138
methods, 5–6, 9–10, 16, 23, 33, 35, 40, 43–45, 55–56, 92–94, 100, 102–103, 106, 108, 118, 132, 143, 158, 161, 164–169
multiple, 5, 19, 22–23, 30, 35, 45–46, 94, 100, 115, 119–120, 122, 124, 126, 133–134, 138, 144, 147–149
reliable, 133, 166
rubrics, 34, 57, 106, 129, 132, 135–136, 139
scoring sheets, 136
summative, 147–148
valid, 127, 133
assignments, 9, 16–18, 22–23, 26, 30, 32–34, 36, 75, 102, 105,109, 120–122, 146–147, 154, 166
concept maps, 44, 101
design of, 9, 35, 42, 141

drafting, 27, 30, 32, 87, 93, 96, 100, 108, 111–112, 114–115
graphics, 78, 82
group, 6, 8, 14, 16, 18, 31, 44, 49, 60–61, 68, 71, 73–76, 78, 85, 88, 95, 105–106, 118–122, 128, 149
individual, 9–10, 31, 42, 70, 77, 98, 101–102, 106, 122, 146, 159, 161, 166, 169
variety in, 47, 167
writing, 4, 10–11, 19–20, 25, 32, 34, 44, 47–49, 68, 73–74, 80, 86, 88, 91, 94, 105, 112, 118–119, 134, 141, 143, 154, 161, 163, 168
atmosphere, *see* classroom environment
attention, 4, 30–31, 43, 46–48, 56, 68, 77–78, 112, 115, 163
selective, 4, 47, 114, 127
attitude, 8, 11, 53–64, 117, 146, 158–160
autonomy, 35, 56–57, 62–64
bar exam, 40, 43, 45, 114
body language, 56, 66
CALI, 46, 50, 168
casebook (textbook), 17, 28–31, 47, 128
cases, 5, 18, 21, 27, 30, 41, 44–48, 70, 92, 104, 112, 115, 117, 120–121, 142
analysis, 46, 75–76, 112, 115, 120, 122

synthesizing, 30
using, 70, 92
challenges, 72, 97–100, 103,
 111, 141, 149, 152, 155, 158
 facing, 72, 93, 100, 131, 151
clarity, 7–8, 11, 34, 162, 165,
 167
class design, 39–40, 49–50,
 103, 113, 122
 checklist, 23, 36, 50, 64, 83,
  89, 108, 123–124, 129,
  132, 135–138, 167, 169
 class preparation, 17, 30, 33,
  147
 classroom, 7, 9, 11–14, 16,
  27, 31, 33, 42, 45, 47, 49,
  65–66, 81–85, 88, 106,
  117, 132, 144, 151, 158,
  160, 164, 166
 context, 5, 17, 27, 36, 39–
  41, 43, 50–51, 54, 57, 61,
  70, 91, 95, 97, 119–121,
  158, 160
  student, 40, 50
  teacher, 40, 50
class planning, 39–40, 43, 46
class sessions, 9–10, 26, 39–40,
 46, 54, 70, 72, 113, 121, 134,
 161
 addressing controversial
  topics, 149
 body of class, 85
 closings, 69, 86, 89
 material, 20, 47
 objectives, 41–50, 70, 87,
 openings, 68–69, 89

classroom assessment
 techniques, 12, 132
 minute papers, 118
classroom environment, 66, 151
 addressing controversial
  issues, 151
closing, 36, 43, 45–46, 49–50,
 69, 72, 85–88, 104
 end of class, 105
closure, 11
clothing, 84
coaching, 63, 131, 166, 169
cognitive, 3–4, 6, 61, 63
 learning theory, 3, 5–6, 158
 processing, 3–4, 30, 49
 strategy, 11, 21, 45, 62, 64,
  71, 99, 115, 117, 129–
  130, 138, 157
communication, 42, 66, 98,
 115, 150, 165–167
competency, 3, 134, 139
concept maps, 44, 101
connections, 20, 62, 98
constructivist learning theory, 5
control, 6, 35, 53–54, 57, 103,
 151, 168
 in the classroom, 9, 11, 14,
  16, 42, 47, 49, 65–66, 81,
  83–85, 88, 144, 151, 158,
  160
cooperative learning, 5, 11, 55
course design, 9, 25–26, 29,
 35–36, 40, 46, 166
 checklist, 23, 36, 50, 64, 83,
  89, 108, 123–124, 129,
  132, 135–138, 167, 169

course webpage, 25, 33–36, 56, 70, 121

feedback, *see* feedback

grading, 33–35, 133–138, 147–148

learning, *see* learning

pacing, 9, 167

policies, 33–35, 71, 96, 98, 115, 117–118

process, 3–6, 16, 25–26, 28, 31, 35–36, 39, 44, 49–50, 54, 56–58, 61–63, 73, 79–81, 83, 92, 113, 121, 123, 125, 133, 135–138, 143-144, 150, 153, 158, 160–161, 164–165

syllabus, 17, 25–26, 31–36, 143–145, 154

course planning, 29

coverage, 29, 35, 41

course, 35

subject matter, 7, 9, 11, 17, 66, 112

discovery sequence instruction, 69, 84

diversity, 58, 99

drafting, 27, 30, 32, 87, 93, 96, 100, 108, 111–112, 114–115

dress, 82–83, 128

email, 7, 48, 70, 93, 96, 99, 135, 142–143, 154

enrollment, 40

enthusiasm, 9, 19–20, 34, 64, 67, 69, 86, 160, 164–165, 168

examples, 11, 20, 30, 37, 44, 47, 51, 64, 84, 86–87, 90, 92–101, 107–109, 111, 115,

118–120, 122, 125, 131–132, 135, 138, 143, 149, 170

use of, 86, 92, 95–97, 99, 107, 132, 138,

expectations, 7–9, 13, 20, 32–33, 35–36, 102, 104–105, 108, 116–117, 135, 144, 150, 152, 154, 160, 165

student, 35

teacher, 8

experiential, 64, 73, 91–109

exercises and methods, 92, 102–103

designing, 102–103, 105

examples of, 64, 84, 92, 94–97, 99, 101, 107–108

teaching and learning, 7–11, 13–23, 43–44, 46, 49, 71, 91–109, 113, 116–117, 124, 157–159, 161–162, 164–166, 168–169

expertise, 7, 55–56, 60, 66, 82, 114, 153, 166

experts, 22, 31, 54, 58, 60, 66, 93, 166

feedback, 7, 9–12, 19, 21, 23, 30, 40, 42, 45–47, 49–50, 55, 58, 63, 78–79, 94, 102, 106, 108, 113, 121–127, 129–130, 132–135, 138, 143, 147–148, 157–158, 160, 162–169

flow, 44, 47, 49, 54, 57, 167

focus questions, 48

formative feedback, 7, 11–12, 46, 113, 121–124, 148, 158, 162–163, 166, 169 fun, 22, 161

grading, 33–35, 133–138, 147–148

groups, 5–6, 11, 18, 70, 75–77, 87, 96, 99, 101–102, 118, 122, 146, 149–150, 152

accountability, 6

assignments, 9, 16–18, 22–23, 26, 30, 32–34, 36, 75, 102, 105, 109, 120–122, 146–147, 154, 166

formal, 8, 71, 84

large, 11, 29, 44, 67, 75–76, 91, 113, 118, 120–122, 148

size, 40, 128

handouts, 44, 47–50, 79, 134

humility, 112, 116

humor, 34, 82, 129, 146

hypotheticals, 18, 21, 30, 44, 46, 49, 102, 118, 128

instructional activities, 40, 42–43, 45, 47, 50, 68, 73–74, 77, 85, 89

instructional design, 158

internet, 50, 78

knowledge, 3, 5, 8, 20, 25, 28, 30, 35, 41–42, 44–45, 50, 83, 99, 104–105, 114–115, 117, 124, 125, 129, 138, 148, 153, 157–158, 165, 168

law practice, 5, 23, 30, 40, 42, 44, 62, 97, 111–112

learner-centered, 50

learning, 3–23, 27–31, 34–35, 39–41, 43–47, 49–50, 53–58, 61–63, 65–75, 77–80, 85–89, 91–109, 111–139, 142, 147–151, 153, 155, 157–162, 164–166, 168

active, 4–5, 7, 10, 40, 56, 68, 73–74, 77–78, 105, 118, 160

activities, 4, 5, 9, 11, 30, 46, 49, 50, 54–55, 57, 77, 105, 113, 117–122, 124, 147

deep, 30, 69, 73, 108, 111–124, 151, 164

exceptional, 111–112, 124

lasting, 92, 111–124

objectives, 35, 45, 65, 72, 77, 80, 85–86, 89, 108, 113–117, 119, 124–125, 136, 151

retrieving, 3

rich, 113, 117–118, 120, 122, 124

storing, 3, 5

textured, 113, 117, 119–120, 122, 124

learning goals, 6, 27, 29, 57, 65, 69, 75, 103, 114, 116–117, 121, 128, 149, 155

learning objectives, 35, 65, 72, 77, 80, 85–86, 89, 108, 113–117, 124–125, 138

learning styles, 44

lectures, 68, 77–78, 89, 101, 117

mini-, 78, 85

listening, 10, 19, 56, 66, 73, 95, 106, 115, 150, 152

mastery, 3, 58

materials, 5, 10, 17–18, 30–31, 42, 47–50, 55, 57, 69, 76, 98, 104, 106, 135, 166
  characteristics of, 60, 121
  focus devices, 48
  functions, 47, 49
  interactive, 3, 47–49, 102
memory, 4, 44
  long-term, 4
  retrieving, 3
  storing, 3, 5
  working, 4, 9, 16, 18, 69–70, 75, 97, 99, 158, 164, 169
models, 18, 31, 61–62, 64, 158
  teachers as, 55, 146
motivation, 8, 10, 40, 42, 53–64, 116, 157–159
  extrinsic, 54, 63
  intrinsic, 54, 58, 63, 157
names, 7, 13–14, 23, 66–67, 70–71, 77, 79, 89, 95, 129, 146
  name cards, 66–67
  name tents, 14
  on exams, 135, 154
nonverbal behavior, 9, 167
novice learners, 79
organization, 9, 42, 44, 162, 165, 167
passion, 7, 9, 43, 55, 64, 112, 116, 147, 160, 164–165, 168
perspectives, 5, 11, 13–23, 53, 111, 117, 150–151
planning, 9–10, 29, 32, 36, 39–40, 43, 46, 146, 150, 161
  assessment, 5, 12, 25, 28–29, 35–36, 45–46
pleadings, 30, 44, 93

policies, 33–35, 71, 96, 98, 115, 117–118
  class, 145,
  course, 33, 35
PowerPoint, 48, 80, 82–83
practice of law, 20, 134
preferences, 10, 16, 27, 34, 44, 71, 74, 128, 161
  learning, 16, 27, 31, 71, 74
preparation, 7, 9, 17, 30, 33, 47–48, 50, 78, 102, 106, 108, 116, 142, 147, 152, 155, 165
  teacher, 102, 108
problem-solving, 36
  engaging students, 4, 57
professional development, 157
  identity, 112–113, 115–116, 124
professionalism, 7, 10, 32, 42, 53, 58, 61–62, 64, 84, 109, 112, 115–116, 124, 139, 154
questions, 11, 18–19, 29, 47–49, 56, 65, 70, 74, 77, 79–80, 82–83, 93, 98, 101, 104, 106–107, 111, 114, 118, 123, 127, 132, 134–136, 141, 148–149, 153, 164–165, 167
  on exams, 135, 154
  on quizzes, 46
reading assignments, 18, 30, 102, 120
  length, 80, 128, 149
  preparation, 7, 9, 17, 30, 33, 47–48, 50, 78, 102, 106, 108, 116, 142, 147, 152, 155, 165
real world experiences, 6
recall, 5, 145

reflection, 12, 49–50, 58, 64, 71, 89, 102, 107–108, 116, 118–120, 122–123, 138–139, 158–160, 162–163, 168–170
students, 108, 120,
reinforcement, 9, 22, 57–58, 61, 64
research, 3, 5–6, 11, 25, 30, 42, 45, 47, 58, 60, 81, 93–95, 98–99, 101, 103, 105–106, 111, 115, 157, 160, 162
respect, 5–7, 13–15, 23, 35–36, 42, 58, 60, 67–69, 82, 85, 99, 116–117, 146, 151, 153, 155, 164
roadmap, 11, 17
role-plays, 108, 126
scholarship, 158
selection, 29, 73
sequencing, 29, 31, 57
pacing, 9, 167
simulations, 5, 10, 16, 43–44, 73, 76, 91, 94, 100, 108, 126, 128
skills, 3, 5, 7–8, 10–11, 20, 25, 27–28, 30, 35, 40–43, 45–46, 48, 50, 70–71, 79, 85, 87, 91, 94, 96, 98–99, 104–105, 111–112, 114–115, 117, 120, 124–125, 128, 134, 138, 148, 157, 166–167
Socratic, 10, 19, 23, 43–44, 57, 74, 79, 120
stress, 72, 84, 88, 116, 127
student, 5–11, 13–23, 28, 31, 34–35, 39–44, 46–50, 53–66, 71, 73–77, 79–82, 88, 93–95, 98–102, 105–108, 116–117, 119–123, 125–139, 142–153, 157–158, 160, 162–163, 165–170
conferences, 141, 168–169
disrespectful, 143–145, 149
evaluations, 145–147, 162–163, 169
interactions, 144
performance, 9, 11, 22, 46, 130
perspective, 14, 27, 98, 167
unmotivated, 141
unprepared, 106, 141–143
student evaluation, 145–147, 162–163, 169
summarizing, 17, 46, 78, 85–86, 98, 123, 152
summative feedback, 148
syllabus, 17, 25–26, 31–36, 143–145, 154
teaching, 1, 3–23, 25, 28–29, 31, 33, 35, 39–40, 43–44, 46, 49–50, 54–58, 61, 64–109, 113, 116–117, 124, 132, 138, 141, 143–146, 153–155, 157–169
collaborative, 113, 116–117, 124
conferences, 141, 168–169
consultant, 12, 158, 163, 166, 168–169
development, 8, 11–12, 54, 58, 62, 95, 111–112, 157–163, 165–169
individual coaching, 166, 169
inventories, 160, 169
journal, 35, 104, 107, 126, 128, 139, 160–162, 169

observations, 159, 165–166
peer review, 139
philosophy, 33, 158–160,
	165, 168
reflection, 12, 49–50, 58, 64,
	71, 89, 102, 107–108, 116,
	118–120, 122–123, 138–
	139, 158–160, 162–163,
	168–170
resources, 9, 37, 47, 51, 64,
	90–91, 101, 108, 132,
	138, 158, 162, 165, 170
support, 3, 5, 7–9, 47, 76,
	82, 88, 115
team, 98
workshops, 141, 168–169
technology, 69, 83, 158
graphics, 78, 82
PowerPoint, 48, 80, 82–83
textbook, 28–29
theory, 3, 5–7, 25, 30, 42, 45,
	48, 50, 111, 114–115, 117,
	119–120, 158, 161–162
think-write-pair-share, 73
thinking, 7, 9–11, 26–28, 31,
	39, 42, 50, 55, 73–74, 78–79,
	81, 115, 141–142, 150, 152,
	160, 169
critical, 11, 42, 79, 115

exercises, 9–10, 16, 18, 47,
	55, 64, 68–69, 71, 73–74,
	90–92, 94, 96, 102–104,
	107
timing, 69, 85, 89
during class, 10, 47, 49, 166
waiting, 142, 152
transfer, 45, 62
troubleshooting, 141–155
values, 10–11, 20, 25, 28, 35,
	41–42, 45–46, 48, 50, 53,
	58, 61–62, 91, 112, 114–117,
	124–125, 128, 138
assessing, 9, 27–28, 35, 46,
	106, 122, 125–139, 147,
	157, 166
practicing, 42, 73, 91, 104–
	105, 115
teaching, 53, 58
variety, 7, 10, 12, 16, 23, 31, 40,
	47, 54, 56, 64, 71, 74, 86, 89,
	91–92, 97–100, 108, 132–
	134, 138, 146, 167
videos, 44, 47–48, 50, 93, 117,
	158, 162, 168
use in class, 48, 50
use of, 47–48, 120, 122, 165
visuals, 11, 69, 77–78, 82, 89
vulnerability, 165